AF679391

Mastery in Azure DevOps: Navigating the Future of Software Development

Kameron Hussain and Frahaan Hussain

Published by Sonar Publishing, 2024.

While every precaution has been taken in the preparation of this book, the publisher assumes no responsibility for errors or omissions, or for damages resulting from the use of the information contained herein.

MASTERY IN AZURE DEVOPS: NAVIGATING THE FUTURE OF SOFTWARE DEVELOPMENT

First edition. March 10, 2024.

Copyright © 2024 Kameron Hussain and Frahaan Hussain.

ISBN: 979-8224560493

Written by Kameron Hussain and Frahaan Hussain.

Table of Contents

Chapter 1: Introduction to Azure DevOps

1.1. The Evolution of DevOps and the Rise of Azure

DevOps, short for Development and Operations, is a set of practices and cultural philosophies that aims to bridge the gap between software development and IT operations teams. It focuses on improving collaboration, automation, and the continuous delivery of high-quality software. DevOps emerged as a response to the challenges posed by traditional software development and deployment practices, which often involved siloed teams, manual processes, and lengthy release cycles.

The Need for DevOps

Before the rise of DevOps, software development and IT operations were often seen as separate entities within an organization. Developers were responsible for writing code, while operations teams were tasked with deploying and managing the infrastructure where the software ran. This division often led to inefficiencies, communication gaps, and a lack of agility in responding to changing business requirements.

Key Challenges in Traditional Practices

1. **Slow Release Cycles:** Traditional software development often followed a waterfall model, where each phase of development, testing, and deployment was sequential. This approach resulted in long release cycles, making it difficult to respond quickly to customer feedback or market

demands.
2. **Manual Processes:** Many tasks in the software development lifecycle were performed manually, such as building and deploying applications, configuring servers, and handling updates. These manual processes were error-prone and time-consuming.
3. **Lack of Collaboration:** Developers and operations teams often worked in isolation, with limited interaction and communication. This lack of collaboration hindered the ability to resolve issues quickly and deliver software efficiently.

The Birth of DevOps

DevOps emerged as a solution to these challenges. It advocates for a culture of collaboration, automation, and continuous improvement. By breaking down the barriers between development and operations, organizations can achieve the following benefits:

- **Faster Delivery:** DevOps practices enable organizations to release software updates and features more frequently, reducing time-to-market.

- **Improved Quality:** Automation and continuous testing help ensure that software is of high quality and free of defects.

- **Enhanced Collaboration:** DevOps fosters a culture of collaboration and shared responsibility, bringing development and operations teams together.

- **Efficient Resource Utilization:** Automation allows for the efficient provisioning and management of infrastructure resources, optimizing costs.

Azure as a DevOps Enabler

Microsoft Azure, a cloud computing platform and service offered by Microsoft, has played a significant role in the evolution of DevOps. Azure provides a wide range of services and tools that support the principles and practices of DevOps, making it easier for organizations to adopt and implement DevOps workflows.

Azure DevOps Services, formerly known as Visual Studio Team Services (VSTS) and Team Foundation Server (TFS), is a comprehensive set of tools and services that cover various aspects of the DevOps lifecycle. It includes capabilities for version control, continuous integration and delivery (CI/CD), project management, testing, and more.

Conclusion

In summary, DevOps represents a fundamental shift in the way organizations approach software development and deployment. It addresses the challenges of traditional practices by promoting collaboration, automation, and continuous delivery. Azure DevOps Services provides a powerful platform for implementing DevOps practices, enabling organizations to streamline their workflows and deliver high-quality software more efficiently. In the following sections of this book, we will delve deeper into Azure DevOps and explore its key concepts and principles.

1.2. Key Concepts and Principles of Azure DevOps

Azure DevOps encompasses a set of key concepts and principles that form the foundation for successful DevOps practices. These concepts and principles guide organizations in their journey towards achieving efficient, collaborative, and automated software development and delivery processes.

Continuous Integration (CI)

Continuous Integration is a fundamental DevOps principle that emphasizes the integration of code changes into a shared repository multiple times a day. Developers frequently commit their code changes, and automated build and testing processes are triggered to verify the integrity of the code. CI helps detect issues early in the development process, ensuring that the codebase remains stable.

In Azure DevOps, you can set up CI pipelines using Azure Pipelines, which automatically build and test your code whenever changes are pushed to a repository. This ensures that your software is continuously validated and ready for deployment.

Continuous Deployment (CD)

Continuous Deployment extends CI by automatically deploying code changes to production or staging environments once they pass the automated tests. CD aims to reduce manual intervention in the deployment process, making it faster and more reliable. Azure DevOps supports CD through Azure Pipelines, allowing you to define deployment workflows and automate the release process.

Infrastructure as Code (IaC)

Infrastructure as Code is a practice that involves defining and managing infrastructure using code, such as templates or scripts. Azure Resource Manager (ARM) templates enable you to define your infrastructure in a declarative manner, making it versionable, repeatable, and automated. IaC ensures that your infrastructure is consistent and can be easily replicated across environments.

Version Control

Version control is crucial for managing source code and tracking changes. Azure DevOps offers version control solutions, including Git and Team Foundation Version Control (TFVC). Git is a distributed version control system that allows for collaboration, branching, and merging of code changes. TFVC is a centralized version control system that provides a structured approach to versioning.

Automated Testing

Automated testing is essential for maintaining code quality and reliability. Azure DevOps supports various testing frameworks and tools, enabling you to automate unit tests, integration tests, and UI tests. Test automation can be integrated into your CI/CD pipelines, ensuring that code changes are thoroughly tested before deployment.

Collaboration and Communication

Effective collaboration and communication are core principles of DevOps. Azure DevOps provides collaboration tools such as Azure Boards for project management, Azure Repos for version control, and Azure Pipelines for CI/CD. Additionally, integration with communication tools like Microsoft Teams and Slack enhances team communication and coordination.

Monitoring and Feedback

Continuous monitoring of applications and infrastructure is critical for identifying issues and gathering feedback. Azure DevOps integrates with Azure Monitor and Application Insights to provide real-time visibility into application performance, error tracking, and usage analytics. Monitoring data can be used to drive improvements and inform future development efforts.

Security and Compliance

Security and compliance are integral to DevOps practices. Azure DevOps incorporates security features such as role-based access control (RBAC), security scanning, and secrets management using Azure Key Vault. Compliance policies can be enforced through Azure Policy, ensuring that deployments adhere to organizational standards and regulatory requirements.

DevOps Culture

DevOps is not just about tools and processes; it's also about fostering a culture of collaboration, trust, and continuous improvement. DevOps culture encourages teams to take ownership of their work, share responsibilities, and learn from failures. It promotes a mindset of collaboration between development and operations, breaking down silos and driving innovation.

Conclusion

These key concepts and principles lay the groundwork for effective DevOps practices in Azure DevOps. As organizations embrace these principles, they can build a culture of collaboration, automation, and continuous improvement that leads to faster, more reliable software delivery and better alignment with business goals. In the subsequent chapters of this book, we will explore how to apply these principles in practice within the Azure DevOps ecosystem.

1.3. Overview of Azure DevOps Services

Azure DevOps Services is a comprehensive cloud-based platform provided by Microsoft to support the entire DevOps lifecycle. It offers a set of tools and services that enable organizations to plan, develop, test, deliver, and monitor software applications seamlessly. In this section, we will provide an overview of Azure DevOps Services and its key components.

Azure DevOps Services Components

Azure DevOps Services comprises several key components, each tailored to specific aspects of the DevOps process:

1. **Azure Boards:** Azure Boards is a work tracking system that helps teams plan, track, and discuss work across the development lifecycle. It supports Agile methodologies and provides features for managing user stories, tasks, bugs, and more. Teams can create and prioritize backlogs, track progress using boards, and visualize work using dashboards.
2. **Azure Repos:** Azure Repos is a version control system that offers Git and Team Foundation Version Control (TFVC) repositories. Git is a distributed version control system that enables collaborative code development, branching, and merging. TFVC is a centralized version control system that provides structure and security for versioning code.
3. **Azure Pipelines:** Azure Pipelines is a CI/CD platform that automates building, testing, and deploying code changes. It supports various programming languages, platforms, and deployment targets. You can define and customize build and release pipelines to fit your project's needs. Azure Pipelines also integrates with

containerization technologies like Docker and Kubernetes.

4. **Azure Test Plans:** Azure Test Plans is a testing toolset that allows teams to plan, track, and manage testing efforts. It supports manual and automated testing, enabling teams to create test plans, test suites, and test cases. Test automation can be integrated into CI/CD pipelines for continuous testing.
5. **Azure Artifacts:** Azure Artifacts is a package management system for managing and hosting package dependencies, such as NuGet, npm, and Maven packages. It facilitates versioning and sharing of packages across teams, ensuring consistent and reliable software builds.
6. **Azure DevOps Boards:** Azure DevOps Boards provides project management and work tracking capabilities that help teams plan, track, and discuss work across the development lifecycle. It supports various Agile methodologies, including Scrum and Kanban, and provides features for backlog management, sprint planning, and reporting.

Integration and Collaboration

One of the strengths of Azure DevOps Services is its integration with a wide range of development and DevOps tools. It seamlessly integrates with popular IDEs (Integrated Development Environments) such as Visual Studio and Visual Studio Code, enabling developers to work within their preferred development environment while leveraging Azure DevOps Services for version control, build, and release pipelines.

Additionally, Azure DevOps Services supports integration with popular collaboration tools like Microsoft Teams and Slack. This integration enhances communication and collaboration among team members, allowing them to stay updated on project progress and receive notifications directly within their communication channels.

Extensibility and Marketplace

Azure DevOps Services is highly extensible, allowing organizations to customize and extend its functionality to meet specific requirements. The Azure DevOps Marketplace offers a wide range of extensions and integrations developed by both Microsoft and third-party vendors. These extensions can enhance the capabilities of Azure DevOps Services in areas such as continuous integration, deployment, monitoring, and more.

Security and Compliance

Microsoft takes security and compliance seriously in Azure DevOps Services. It provides a range of security features, including role-based access control (RBAC), secure access to repositories, and compliance with industry standards and certifications such as ISO 27001, SOC 2, and HIPAA. Teams can enforce security policies and access controls to protect their code and data.

Conclusion

Azure DevOps Services is a powerful and versatile platform that empowers organizations to adopt DevOps practices effectively. Its integrated tools and services cover the entire DevOps lifecycle, from planning and development to testing and deployment. In the subsequent chapters of this book, we will dive deeper into each of these components and explore how to leverage them for successful DevOps implementation.

1.4. The Importance of Azure DevOps in

Modern Software Engineering

Azure DevOps has become a cornerstone in modern software engineering, playing a pivotal role in enabling organizations to stay competitive, deliver high-quality software, and respond to market demands rapidly. In this section, we will explore the significance of Azure DevOps in today's software development landscape.

Accelerating Time-to-Market

In the digital age, speed is of the essence. Organizations need to bring new features and products to market swiftly to meet customer expectations and stay ahead of competitors. Azure DevOps, with its robust CI/CD capabilities, empowers teams to automate and streamline the software delivery process. This automation significantly reduces the time required to develop, test, and deploy software, enabling faster releases and updates.

Enhancing Collaboration

Collaboration is a fundamental aspect of successful software development. Azure DevOps fosters collaboration by providing a centralized platform for teams to work together. Developers, testers, and operations professionals can collaborate seamlessly within the same environment, improving communication and ensuring that everyone is aligned toward common goals.

Ensuring Quality and Reliability

Quality and reliability are non-negotiable in today's software landscape. Azure DevOps encourages a culture of continuous testing and automation, which helps identify and rectify issues early in the development cycle. Automated testing, integrated with CI/CD pipelines, ensures that each code change is thoroughly tested, reducing the likelihood of introducing defects into production.

Adapting to Change

Change is a constant in software development. Customer feedback, market dynamics, and technology advancements necessitate frequent updates and adaptations. Azure DevOps provides the flexibility and agility required to respond to change swiftly. It supports feature flags and feature toggles, allowing organizations to release new features gradually and experiment with different configurations.

Optimizing Resource Utilization

Efficient resource utilization is critical for cost-effectiveness. Azure DevOps helps organizations optimize resource usage by automating the provisioning and scaling of infrastructure. With Infrastructure as Code (IaC) and containerization, teams can create and manage resources efficiently, reducing operational overhead and costs.

Increasing Visibility and Insights

Azure DevOps offers robust monitoring and reporting capabilities. Teams can gain insights into the performance and health of applications through Azure Monitor and Application Insights. These tools provide real-time visibility, enabling teams to proactively address issues and make data-driven decisions.

Scalability and Elasticity

Modern applications need to scale both up and down based on demand. Azure DevOps supports the creation of scalable and elastic architectures, allowing applications to handle fluctuations in traffic seamlessly. Auto-scaling, container orchestration, and serverless computing are some of the techniques that can be leveraged.

Compliance and Security

Security and compliance are paramount concerns in software engineering. Azure DevOps incorporates security features and practices, such as RBAC, secure code scanning, and secrets management. It also enables organizations to enforce compliance policies and adhere to industry regulations.

Conclusion

In summary, Azure DevOps is not just a set of tools; it represents a transformational approach to modern software engineering. Its impact is far-reaching, from accelerating time-to-market and enhancing collaboration to ensuring quality, adapting to change, and optimizing resource utilization. Azure DevOps is a critical enabler for organizations striving to deliver high-quality software products in an agile and competitive landscape. As we delve deeper into the chapters of this book, we will explore how to harness the power of Azure DevOps to address these imperatives effectively.

1.5. Setting Up for Success: Prerequisites and Initial Setup

Before diving into the practical aspects of Azure DevOps, it's essential to lay a strong foundation by addressing the prerequisites and performing the initial setup. This section will guide you through the necessary steps to ensure a smooth start with Azure DevOps.

Prerequisites

1. Azure Subscription

To leverage Azure DevOps, you'll need an Azure subscription. If you don't already have one, you can sign up for a free Azure account or an Azure DevOps account, both of which provide a limited amount of free resources to get started.

2. Azure DevOps Account

You'll need an Azure DevOps account to access the platform's services. You can sign up for a free Azure DevOps account or use an existing one if your organization already has one set up.

3. Development Environment

Ensure that your development environment is set up and ready. This includes having the necessary software tools, such as an integrated development environment (IDE) like Visual Studio or Visual Studio Code, installed on your development machine.

4. Source Code

If you're working on an existing project, make sure you have access to the source code. If you're starting a new project, create a codebase or repository where you'll store your code.

5. Azure DevOps Organization

Within your Azure DevOps account, create or join an organization. An organization in Azure DevOps is a container for projects, teams, and resources. It helps you structure your work and collaborate effectively.

Initial Setup

1. Creating a Project

Once you have your Azure DevOps organization set up, the first step is to create a project. A project is a container for your software development efforts. You can choose a project name, description, and visibility settings according to your organization's needs.

2. Defining a Version Control Strategy

Decide on your version control strategy. Azure DevOps supports both Git and Team Foundation Version Control (TFVC). Git is a popular choice for its distributed and collaborative nature. Create a Git repository within your project to manage your source code.

3. Setting Up Build and Release Pipelines

Azure DevOps provides powerful CI/CD capabilities through Azure Pipelines. You'll need to set up build and release pipelines to automate the building, testing, and deployment of your software. Define the build steps, testing frameworks, and deployment targets in your pipelines.

4. Managing Work Items

Azure DevOps offers Azure Boards for work item management. Define and manage your backlog, user stories, tasks, and bugs within

Azure Boards. This helps track progress and prioritize work effectively.

5. Configuring Permissions

Security is crucial. Configure permissions and access control to ensure that only authorized users can access and modify resources within your Azure DevOps project. Use role-based access control (RBAC) to manage permissions.

6. Integrating with Development Tools

Integrate Azure DevOps with your preferred development tools, such as Visual Studio or Visual Studio Code. These integrations enable a seamless development experience and streamline interactions with Azure DevOps.

7. Setting Up Monitoring and Alerts

Consider setting up monitoring and alerts using Azure Monitor and Application Insights to gain visibility into your application's performance and health. Configure alerts to be notified of issues promptly.

8. Defining Coding Standards

Establish coding standards and guidelines within your development team. This ensures consistent code quality and makes it easier to maintain and review code changes.

Conclusion

Setting up for success in Azure DevOps involves addressing prerequisites and performing initial configurations. By following these steps, you'll create a strong foundation for your DevOps journey, enabling your team to work efficiently, deliver high-quality software, and collaborate effectively throughout the development lifecycle. In the subsequent chapters, we will explore each aspect of Azure DevOps in more detail, providing hands-on guidance and best practices for successful implementation.

Chapter 2: Azure Boards - Agile Project Management

2.1. Introduction to Azure Boards

Azure Boards is a powerful Agile project management tool within Azure DevOps Services that helps teams plan, track, and manage work effectively. Whether you follow Scrum, Kanban, or custom Agile methodologies, Azure Boards provides the flexibility and features to support your project management needs. In this section, we'll introduce you to the core concepts and capabilities of Azure Boards.

Work Items

At the heart of Azure Boards are work items. Work items represent individual tasks, user stories, bugs, or any other unit of work that needs to be managed within your project. Each work item has a unique identifier, a title, and a set of fields to capture relevant information.

Work items can be categorized into various types, such as:

- **User Stories:** Represent customer or user requirements, typically in the form of features or functionality.
- **Tasks:** Break down user stories into smaller, actionable items that team members can work on.
- **Bugs:** Track issues or defects that need to be addressed.
- **Epics:** High-level containers for grouping related user stories and tasks.

- **Features:** Higher-level work items that encompass multiple user stories.

Boards

Azure Boards provides customizable boards that help teams visualize and manage work items. Two primary types of boards are available:

- **Kanban Boards:** Ideal for teams practicing Kanban methodologies. Kanban boards provide a visual representation of work items as cards that move through various columns, representing different stages of work (e.g., To Do, In Progress, Done).

- **Sprint Boards:** Suited for teams following Scrum. Sprint boards help plan and manage work for a specific time frame, known as a sprint. Work items are organized into a sprint backlog and can be tracked using burndown charts.

Backlogs

Backlogs in Azure Boards allow you to prioritize and plan work items. There are two main types of backlogs:

- **Product Backlog:** Contains all the work items that need to be completed over time. This backlog is often managed by the product owner and serves as a source for selecting items to include in future sprints.

- **Sprint Backlog:** Focuses on the work items planned for a specific sprint in Scrum. Sprint backlogs help the team understand what needs to be accomplished during the sprint.

Agile Methodologies

Azure Boards supports various Agile methodologies, including Scrum, Kanban, and custom approaches. You can choose the methodology that best suits your team's needs and customize your boards, backlogs, and workflows accordingly.

Work Item Tracking

Work item tracking in Azure Boards involves the entire lifecycle of work items, from creation to completion. Teams can update work item statuses, assign tasks to team members, link work items to related items, and add comments to facilitate communication and collaboration.

Queries and Reporting

Azure Boards provides robust querying and reporting capabilities. You can create custom queries to filter and retrieve work items based on criteria such as work item type, priority, or assigned team member. Reports and dashboards help teams monitor progress and make data-driven decisions.

Integrations

Azure Boards seamlessly integrates with other Azure DevOps Services, including Azure Repos (for version control) and Azure Pipelines (for CI/CD). This integration ensures that work items are linked to code changes and builds, providing traceability and visibility into the development process.

Conclusion

Azure Boards is a versatile Agile project management tool that empowers teams to plan, track, and manage work efficiently.

Whether your team follows Scrum, Kanban, or a custom Agile approach, Azure Boards provides the flexibility and features to support your project management needs. In the following sections, we will explore how to set up and use Azure Boards effectively within your Azure DevOps project.

2.2. Managing Work Items and Backlogs

Managing work items and backlogs effectively is essential for successful Agile project management in Azure Boards. In this section, we'll delve into the details of how to create, update, and prioritize work items, as well as how to manage your product and sprint backlogs.

Creating Work Items

To start managing work items, you need to create them. Follow these steps to create a new work item in Azure Boards:

1. **Navigate to Your Project:** Access your Azure DevOps project and choose the appropriate board, either Kanban or Sprint, depending on your methodology.
2. **Select "New Work Item":** Look for the "New Work Item" button, usually located near the top of the board.
3. **Choose Work Item Type:** Select the type of work item you want to create, such as User Story, Task, Bug, or any custom types you've defined.
4. **Fill in Details:** Provide a title, description, and any other necessary information for the work item. You can specify the area, iteration, and assign it to team members.
5. **Save the Work Item:** Once you've filled in the required information, save the work item.

Updating Work Items

Work items are not static; they evolve as the project progresses. Azure Boards allows you to update work items to reflect changes and progress. Here's how to update work items:

1. **Select the Work Item:** Locate the work item you want to update on your board or in a backlog.
2. **Edit the Work Item:** Open the work item and click on the "Edit" button. You can make changes to the title, description, assigned team members, state, and other fields.
3. **Save Changes:** After making your updates, save the changes to the work item.
4. **Add Comments:** Consider adding comments to provide additional context or communicate with team members regarding the work item.

Prioritizing Work Items

Prioritization is crucial for ensuring that the most valuable work items are addressed first. In Azure Boards, you can prioritize work items by adjusting their order in the backlog. Here's how to do it:

1. **Access the Backlog:** Navigate to the appropriate backlog (Product or Sprint) for your project.
2. **Drag and Drop:** Work items in the backlog can usually be dragged and dropped to change their order. This action represents their prioritization.
3. **Use Stack Rank or Priority Fields:** Some teams prefer using fields like "Stack Rank" or "Priority" to explicitly indicate the order of work items. You can update these fields to reflect priorities.

Product Backlog

The Product Backlog is a central repository for all work items related to the project. It helps product owners, stakeholders, and teams plan and prioritize upcoming work. To effectively manage the Product Backlog:

- Regularly review and groom the backlog to ensure it reflects the most valuable and current work items.

- Collaborate with stakeholders to gather input and refine the backlog.

- Break down larger items, such as epics or features, into smaller user stories or tasks for better manageability.

Sprint Backlog

The Sprint Backlog focuses on the work items that need to be completed during a specific sprint in Scrum. To manage the Sprint Backlog:

- Select work items from the Product Backlog and move them into the Sprint Backlog for the upcoming sprint.

- Ensure that the work items in the Sprint Backlog are well-defined and achievable within the sprint's time frame.

- Monitor progress during the sprint using burndown charts and adjust priorities or work as needed.

Queries and Filters

Azure Boards provides powerful querying and filtering capabilities to help you find and organize work items effectively. You can create custom queries to filter work items based on various criteria, such as work item type, area, iteration, and assigned team member. Queries can be saved and reused for ongoing work item tracking.

Conclusion

Effective management of work items and backlogs is central to Agile project management in Azure Boards. By creating, updating, prioritizing, and organizing work items, teams can maintain visibility into their progress and ensure that the most valuable work is addressed first. In the next sections, we'll explore additional features and best practices for Agile project management using Azure Boards.

2.3. Implementing Agile Methodologies with Azure Boards

Azure Boards is a versatile tool that supports various Agile methodologies, allowing teams to adapt their project management practices to fit their specific needs. In this section, we'll explore how to implement Agile methodologies such as Scrum and Kanban using Azure Boards.

Scrum with Azure Boards

Sprint Planning

In Scrum, work is organized into time-boxed iterations called sprints. To implement Scrum using Azure Boards:

1. **Create a Scrum Team:** Set up a Scrum team within your Azure DevOps project.
2. **Define Sprints:** Define a sprint schedule and create sprints for your project. Sprints typically last 2-4 weeks.
3. **Backlog Refinement:** The Product Owner and the team collaborate to refine and prioritize the Product Backlog. Move selected items to the Sprint Backlog for the upcoming sprint.
4. **Sprint Planning Meeting:** In a sprint planning meeting, the team reviews the selected work items, discusses requirements, and commits to completing a set of tasks during the sprint.
5. **Use Burndown Charts:** Azure Boards provides burndown charts to track progress during the sprint. Keep an eye on the burndown chart to ensure work is on track.

Daily Standup

Scrum teams often hold daily standup meetings to discuss progress and plan the day's work. Azure Boards can be used to facilitate these meetings:

1. **Review Work Items:** During the daily standup, team members can review work items on the Sprint Board to discuss their status and any impediments.
2. **Update Work Items:** Team members can update the state of their assigned work items to reflect progress.
3. **Identify Blockers:** If any blockers or impediments are identified, they can be recorded as work items and assigned for resolution.

Sprint Review and Retrospective

At the end of each sprint, a review and retrospective meeting is conducted. Azure Boards supports these activities:

1. **Review Meeting:** During the sprint review meeting, the team presents completed work to stakeholders. Azure Boards can be used to track and display completed work items.
2. **Retrospective Meeting:** In the retrospective meeting, the team reflects on the sprint and identifies areas for improvement. Use Azure Boards to record and track action items from the retrospective.

Kanban with Azure Boards

Visualizing Work

Kanban is all about visualizing work and managing flow. Azure Boards offers Kanban boards to support these principles:

1. **Create a Kanban Board:** Set up a Kanban board for your team or project.
2. **Work Items as Cards:** Work items are represented as cards on the Kanban board. These cards move through different columns, indicating their progress.
3. **Column Definitions:** Customize columns on the board to represent different stages of work. Common columns include "To Do," "In Progress," and "Done."
4. **Work in Progress (WIP) Limits:** Set WIP limits for columns to manage the flow of work and prevent overloading the team.

Continuous Delivery

Kanban promotes continuous delivery, with a focus on completing work items as soon as they are started. Azure Boards can be configured to support this approach:

1. **Limit Work in Progress:** Enforce WIP limits to encourage the team to finish work before starting new items.
2. **Pull System:** Use a pull system where team members pull work items from the "To Do" column when they have capacity.
3. **Cycle Time:** Monitor cycle time (the time it takes for a work item to move from "To Do" to "Done") to identify bottlenecks and improve efficiency.

Custom Agile Approaches

Azure Boards is highly flexible and can be adapted to custom Agile approaches. Whether your team follows a hybrid model or a unique methodology, you can tailor boards, backlogs, and workflows to suit your needs. Define custom work item types, states, and transitions to match your specific Agile framework.

Conclusion

Azure Boards offers robust support for implementing Agile methodologies such as Scrum and Kanban. Whether you follow these well-established frameworks or have a custom Agile approach, Azure Boards provides the flexibility and tools to adapt your project management practices to your team's requirements. By utilizing the features and customization options available, you can effectively manage your Agile projects and achieve better visibility, collaboration, and delivery outcomes.

2.4. Customizing Boards for Team Efficiency

Azure Boards provides a high degree of customization, allowing teams to tailor their boards to match their unique workflows and requirements. In this section, we'll explore how to customize boards in Azure Boards to enhance team efficiency and productivity.

Board Customization Basics

Customizing your Azure Boards involves modifying the columns, work item types, states, and workflows to align with your team's specific processes. Here are some key aspects of board customization:

Columns:

Columns represent the different stages of work items as they progress through your workflow. Customize the columns to match your team's unique steps. Common columns include "To Do," "In Progress," and "Done."

Work Item Types:

Azure Boards supports various work item types, including User Stories, Tasks, Bugs, Epics, and custom types. Define the types that best suit your project and workflow.

States:

Each work item type has a set of states that represent its lifecycle. Modify these states to match your process. For example, you can define states like "Ready for Review" or "In Testing" for a Task work item.

Workflows:

Workflows define the transitions between states for work item types. Customize workflows to ensure that work items move through your defined process efficiently.

Column Customization

Column customization is a powerful feature in Azure Boards that allows you to adapt your board to your team's workflow. Here's how to customize columns:

1. **Access Board Settings:** Navigate to your board and click on "Board settings" or "Columns."
2. **Add or Remove Columns:** You can add new columns, reorder existing ones, or remove columns that are not relevant to your workflow.
3. **Define WIP Limits:** Implement Work in Progress (WIP) limits on columns to control the number of work items allowed in each stage. This prevents overloading and encourages flow.
4. **Column Mapping:** Map columns to work item states to ensure a seamless transition as work items move through your process.

Swimlanes

Swimlanes provide an additional level of organization on your board. You can create swimlanes based on various criteria, such as team members, work item types, priorities, or custom fields.

Swimlanes help teams categorize and visualize work items more effectively.

Card Styles

Card styles allow you to format work item cards on the board based on specific criteria. For example, you can highlight high-priority items with a different color or style, making them more visible on the board.

Queries and Filters

Queries and filters help teams focus on specific subsets of work items. You can create custom queries to filter work items based on criteria like work item type, area, iteration, and more. These queries can be saved for quick access.

Card Annotations

Card annotations allow you to add additional information to work item cards. This can be useful for displaying important context or details directly on the card without the need to open the work item.

Card Reordering

Azure Boards allows you to reorder cards on the board manually. This feature is particularly useful for teams following Kanban or custom workflows, where the order of work items matters.

Board Widgets

Azure Boards supports the addition of widgets to boards, providing additional information and functionality. Widgets can display data from Azure DevOps or external sources, helping teams access relevant information without leaving the board.

Conclusion

Customizing boards in Azure Boards is essential for tailoring the platform to your team's specific workflow and requirements. By optimizing columns, swimlanes, card styles, and other customization options, you can enhance team efficiency and productivity. Azure Boards provides the flexibility needed to adapt to various Agile methodologies and unique processes, ensuring that your team can work effectively and achieve its project management goals. In the following sections, we'll explore more advanced customization options and best practices to further optimize your boards for efficient project management.

2.5. Reporting and Analytics in Azure Boards

Azure Boards provides powerful reporting and analytics capabilities that allow teams to gain insights into their project's progress, identify bottlenecks, and make data-driven decisions. In this section, we'll explore the reporting and analytics features in Azure Boards.

Query-Based Reporting

Query-based reporting is one of the core features in Azure Boards. It allows teams to create custom queries to filter and retrieve work items based on various criteria. Here's how it works:

1. **Create Queries:** Users can create custom queries to filter work items. Queries can be based on criteria such as work item type, state, area, iteration, assigned team member, and custom fields.
2. **Save and Share Queries:** Once a query is defined, it can be saved for future use. Queries can also be shared with team members, making it easy to collaborate and track

work items.

3. **Dynamic Updates:** Queries are dynamic, meaning they reflect real-time data. As work items are created or updated, the query results automatically update to show the latest information.
4. **Query Hierarchy:** Queries can be organized hierarchically, allowing teams to create complex and structured queries. For example, you can have a parent query that includes several child queries.

Charts and Dashboards

Azure Boards offers a variety of chart types that allow teams to visualize their project's data. These charts can be added to dashboards for easy access. Some of the available chart types include:

- **Burndown and Burnup Charts:** Track progress and visualize remaining work in sprints.

- **Cumulative Flow Diagrams:** Analyze work item flow and identify bottlenecks in the workflow.

- **Velocity Charts:** View historical velocity to better plan future sprints.

- **Lead and Cycle Time Charts:** Measure the time it takes for work items to move through the workflow stages.

- **Custom Charts:** Create custom charts using work item queries to visualize specific metrics and KPIs.

Dashboards are highly customizable, allowing teams to create personalized views that display the most relevant information.

Dashboards can be shared with team members and stakeholders, providing a central place to monitor project progress.

Analytics Views

Azure Boards also provides Analytics Views, which offer advanced reporting capabilities. Analytics Views allow users to define and save complex queries that provide detailed insights into work item data. These views can be used to analyze trends, track historical data, and perform in-depth data exploration.

Power BI Integration

For more advanced reporting and data visualization needs, Azure Boards can be integrated with Microsoft Power BI. Power BI allows teams to create custom reports and dashboards using Azure Boards data. This integration provides greater flexibility in analyzing and presenting project metrics.

REST API for Custom Reporting

Teams looking to build custom reporting solutions can leverage the Azure DevOps REST API. This API allows developers to programmatically access and retrieve work item data for custom reporting and analytics purposes. By using the REST API, teams can create tailored reports and integrate Azure Boards data into their existing tools and workflows.

Conclusion

Reporting and analytics in Azure Boards play a crucial role in helping teams monitor project progress, identify areas for improvement, and make informed decisions. Whether through query-based reporting, built-in charts and dashboards, Analytics

Views, Power BI integration, or custom solutions using the REST API, Azure Boards offers a wide range of options for teams to gain insights and optimize their project management processes. These features empower teams to continuously improve their Agile practices and deliver high-quality software efficiently.

Chapter 3: Azure Repos - Source Control Management

3.1. Understanding Source Control in Azure DevOps

Source control, often referred to as version control or revision control, is a critical component of modern software development. It allows teams to manage changes to their codebase, collaborate effectively, and ensure the integrity and reliability of their software. In this section, we'll delve into the fundamentals of source control in the context of Azure DevOps.

What is Source Control?

Source control is a system that tracks changes to files and directories over time, allowing multiple developers to collaborate on a project concurrently. It provides the following key functionalities:

1. **Versioning:** Source control systems maintain a history of every change made to files, enabling developers to view and revert to previous versions when needed. This version history is invaluable for debugging and auditing.
2. **Concurrency:** Multiple developers can work on the same project simultaneously without conflicts. Source control systems handle merging changes made by different team members.
3. **Collaboration:** Developers can easily collaborate by sharing their code through a centralized repository. This promotes teamwork and ensures that everyone is working on the latest version of the codebase.
4. **Backup and Recovery:** Source control systems act as a

backup for code and project assets. If files are accidentally deleted or corrupted, they can be restored from the repository's history.

Key Concepts in Source Control

To understand source control in Azure DevOps, you need to be familiar with the following essential concepts:

Repository:

A repository is a storage location where all project files and version history are stored. Azure DevOps provides Git and Team Foundation Version Control (TFVC) repositories, allowing teams to choose the version control system that suits their needs.

Branch:

A branch is a separate line of development within a repository. Developers create branches to work on new features, bug fixes, or experiments without affecting the main codebase. Branches can be merged back into the main branch when work is completed.

Commit:

A commit represents a set of changes made to one or more files. Each commit has a unique identifier and includes a commit message that describes the changes. Commits are the building blocks of version history.

Merge:

Merging is the process of combining changes from one branch into another. It is typically used to integrate completed features or bug fixes back into the main branch. Merge conflicts can occur when changes in two branches conflict with each other.

Pull Request (PR):

A pull request is a request to merge changes from one branch into another. It is a common practice to use pull requests for code review and collaboration. During a pull request, team members can review the code, provide feedback, and ensure that the changes meet quality standards before merging.

Fork:

Forking is the process of creating a copy of a repository. It is often used in open-source projects, where contributors create forks of the main repository to work on their changes independently. After making changes in their fork, contributors can submit pull requests to the main repository for review and integration.

Git vs. TFVC

Azure DevOps supports two main version control systems: Git and Team Foundation Version Control (TFVC). Git is a distributed version control system that offers flexibility and branching capabilities. TFVC is a centralized version control system with a more traditional approach. Teams can choose the system that aligns with their development workflow and preferences.

Conclusion

Source control is a fundamental aspect of modern software development, and Azure DevOps provides robust tools and capabilities to manage version control effectively. Understanding the key concepts of repositories, branches, commits, merges, pull requests, and forks is essential for collaborating on projects and maintaining code integrity. Whether your team chooses Git or TFVC, Azure DevOps supports both options to ensure efficient and reliable source control management. In the following sections, we'll dive deeper into setting up and managing repositories and branches within Azure DevOps.

3.2. Setting Up and Managing Repositories

Setting up and managing repositories is a fundamental aspect of source control in Azure DevOps. In this section, we'll explore how to create and configure repositories, as well as best practices for managing them effectively.

Creating a Repository

Azure DevOps provides the flexibility to create multiple repositories within a project, supporting different codebases or components. Here's how to create a new repository:

1. **Access Your Project:** Navigate to your Azure DevOps project where you want to create a repository.
2. **Choose Repos:** In the project's dashboard, select the "Repos" tab to access the repository section.
3. **Create a Repository:** Click the "New" button or equivalent action to create a new repository.
4. **Define Repository Settings:** Provide a name and optional

description for the repository. Choose the version control system (Git or TFVC) that best suits your project.

5. **Access Controls:** Configure access controls and permissions for the repository, specifying who can view, clone, and contribute to it.
6. **Initialize with a README:** You have the option to initialize the repository with a README file, which can serve as initial documentation for your codebase.

Managing Repository Branches

Branches are an essential part of source control, allowing teams to work on different features or fixes simultaneously. Here's how to manage branches in your Azure DevOps repository:

Creating Branches:

1. **Access Repository:** Navigate to your repository within Azure DevOps.
2. **Branch Dropdown:** Look for the "Branch" or "New Branch" dropdown, which allows you to create a new branch based on an existing one or the main branch.
3. **Provide Branch Name:** Give your new branch a meaningful name, such as "feature/my-new-feature" or "bugfix/issue-123."
4. **Create Branch:** Confirm the creation of the new branch. It is now available for development.

Merging Branches:

1. **Pull Request:** To merge changes from one branch into another, create a pull request. Navigate to the "Pull Requests" section in your repository and initiate a new PR.

2. **Select Source and Target Branch:** Specify the source branch (the one with changes) and the target branch (the one to which changes will be merged).
3. **Review and Approve:** Review the changes, add reviewers, and request feedback. Team members can review and approve the PR before merging.
4. **Complete Merge:** Once the PR is approved and all checks pass, complete the merge. The changes are integrated into the target branch.

Deleting Branches:

1. **Branch Management:** Azure DevOps provides branch management features to delete branches that are no longer needed. Be cautious when deleting branches, as it permanently removes them.

Cloning Repositories

To work on a repository locally, developers need to clone it to their development environment. Here's how to clone a repository from Azure DevOps:

1. **Access Repository:** Go to the Azure DevOps repository you want to clone.
2. **Clone Button:** Look for the "Clone" button or equivalent action, which provides the repository's URL.
3. **Use Git Client:** Use a Git client like Git Bash, GitKraken, or Visual Studio Code to clone the repository using the provided URL.
4. **Authentication:** If required, authenticate with your Azure DevOps credentials during the cloning process.

Best Practices for Repository Management

Effective repository management is crucial for maintaining code quality and collaboration. Here are some best practices:

- **Use Descriptive Branch Names:** Choose meaningful branch names that describe the purpose of the branch, such as feature names or issue numbers.

- **Regularly Merge Changes:** Encourage frequent merging of feature branches into the main branch to prevent long-lived branches and merge conflicts.

- **Implement Code Reviews:** Require code reviews for all pull requests to maintain code quality and catch issues early.

- **Protect the Main Branch:** Set up branch protection policies to prevent direct commits to the main branch, ensuring that all changes go through pull requests.

- **Automate Testing:** Implement automated testing and continuous integration (CI) to ensure that changes do not introduce regressions.

- **Document Repository:** Include documentation in your repository, such as a README file, to help developers understand the project and its dependencies.

Conclusion

Setting up and managing repositories is a fundamental step in source control within Azure DevOps. By creating repositories, managing branches, and following best practices, teams can collaborate effectively, maintain code quality, and ensure that changes are integrated smoothly. Effective repository management is a cornerstone of successful software development projects, and Azure DevOps provides the tools and flexibility needed to achieve it. In the following sections, we'll dive deeper into branching strategies, pull requests, and code reviews to enhance the development process.

3.3. Branching and Merging Strategies

Branching and merging are critical aspects of source control in Azure DevOps. They enable teams to manage concurrent development, isolate new features or bug fixes, and ensure code stability. In this section, we'll explore branching and merging strategies that can be employed within Azure DevOps.

Branching Strategies

Choosing the right branching strategy is essential for efficient and organized development. Azure DevOps supports various branching strategies, including:

Feature Branching:

In a feature branching strategy, each new feature or enhancement is developed in a dedicated branch. Once the feature is complete and tested, it is merged back into the main branch. This approach keeps the main branch stable and allows for parallel development of multiple features.

 # Create a new feature branch

git checkout -b feature/my-new-feature

 # Work on the feature, make commits

...

 # Merge the feature branch into the main branch

git checkout main

git merge feature/my-new-feature

Release Branching:

Release branching is suitable for projects with a well-defined release schedule. A release branch is created from the main branch when preparing for a release. Only bug fixes and essential changes are allowed in the release branch. Once the release is ready, it is merged back into both the main branch and any long-term support (LTS) branches.

 # Create a release branch

git checkout -b release/1.0

 # Perform bug fixes and updates for the release

...

 # Merge the release branch into main and LTS branches

git checkout main

git merge release/1.0

Gitflow:

Gitflow is a branching model that defines a structured approach to source control. It involves two main branches, "main" and "develop," along with feature branches, release branches, and hotfix branches.

This model provides a clear workflow for feature development, release preparation, and bug fixing.

```
# Create a new feature branch using Gitflow

git flow feature start my-feature

# Finish the feature and merge it into the develop branch

git flow feature finish my-feature
```

Merging Strategies

Merging changes from one branch into another requires a strategy to ensure code quality and minimize conflicts. Azure DevOps supports different merging strategies:

Regular Merging:

Regular merging is the simplest strategy, where changes are merged from one branch into another without preserving the commit history. This can result in a linear and straightforward history but may make it harder to track where changes originated.

```
# Merge changes from a feature branch into main

git checkout main

git merge feature/my-feature
```

Pull Request Merging:

Pull requests (PRs) are often used for merging changes in Azure DevOps. PRs provide a mechanism for code review, automated testing, and collaboration. When a PR is completed and approved, the changes are merged into the target branch.

 # Create a pull request to merge feature branch into main

 # PR is reviewed, approved, and completed in Azure DevOps

Rebase and Merge:

Rebase and merge is a strategy that preserves the commit history of the source branch while incorporating changes into the target branch. It can result in a more organized and logical commit history.

 # Rebase feature branch on top of main branch

git checkout feature/my-feature

git rebase main

 # Merge the rebased feature branch into main

git checkout main

git merge feature/my-feature

Squash and Merge:

Squash and merge is a strategy where all commits from a source branch are combined into a single commit before merging into the target branch. This can help keep the commit history concise.

 # Squash commits from feature branch into one commit

git checkout feature/my-feature

git reset $(git merge-base feature/my-feature main)

```
git add -A

git commit -m "Add my new feature"

# Merge the squashed commit into main

git checkout main

git merge feature/my-feature
```

Choosing the Right Strategy

The choice of branching and merging strategies depends on the project's complexity, team size, release cadence, and development workflow. It's essential to select a strategy that aligns with your project's needs and ensures code stability and collaboration. Azure DevOps provides the flexibility to implement various strategies and supports a wide range of development scenarios.

Conclusion

Branching and merging strategies are crucial for successful source control management in Azure DevOps. By selecting the appropriate strategy, teams can streamline development, isolate changes, and maintain code quality. Whether you opt for feature branching, release branching, Gitflow, or a combination of strategies, Azure DevOps offers the tools and workflows needed to implement these strategies effectively. In the following sections, we'll explore more advanced topics, such as pull requests, code reviews, and integrations, to enhance the development process further.

3.4. Pull Requests and Code Review Practices

Pull requests (PRs) and code reviews are essential components of a well-managed source control process in Azure DevOps. They play a crucial role in maintaining code quality, ensuring collaboration, and catching issues early. In this section, we'll delve into pull requests and best practices for code reviews within Azure DevOps.

Pull Request Workflow

A pull request is a formal request to merge changes from one branch into another. It serves as a mechanism for code review, feedback, and collaboration among team members. Here's an overview of the typical pull request workflow:

1. **Creating a Pull Request:**

   – Developers create a pull request when they want to merge changes from their feature branch into the main branch or another target branch.

   – During the pull request creation, developers provide a title, description, and list of reviewers.

1. **Review and Feedback:**

   – Reviewers are notified of the pull request and can access the changes made by the developer.

   – Reviewers examine the code, provide feedback, and suggest improvements. They can also comment on specific lines of code.

1. **Iterative Changes:**

   – Developers can make additional changes to the code based on the feedback received from reviewers.

– The iterative process continues until reviewers are satisfied with the changes.

1. **Approval:**

– Once the code meets the quality standards and has been approved by reviewers, the pull request is marked as approved.

1. **Automated Checks:**

– Automated checks, such as continuous integration (CI) tests and code analysis, are often triggered when a pull request is created or updated. These checks help ensure that the code is functional and adheres to coding standards.

1. **Merging:**

– After approval and passing automated checks, the pull request can be merged into the target branch, incorporating the changes into the codebase.

Best Practices for Pull Requests

Effective pull request practices are essential for a smooth and productive development process. Here are some best practices to follow:

Small and Focused PRs:

Create pull requests that focus on specific changes or features. Avoid large and complex PRs that are challenging to review.

Clear Descriptions:

Provide clear and informative descriptions for your pull requests. Explain the purpose of the changes, any related issues or user stories, and the testing approach.

Assign Reviewers:

Assign appropriate reviewers to your pull requests. Reviewers should have the relevant expertise to evaluate the code changes effectively.

Address Feedback:

Be responsive to feedback from reviewers. Address comments, questions, and suggestions promptly and professionally.

Automated Tests:

Ensure that your code changes include automated tests. These tests should cover both new functionality and any modifications to existing code.

Code Quality:

Maintain code quality by adhering to coding standards and best practices. Use code analysis tools and linters to identify and address issues.

Avoid Direct Commits:

Discourage direct commits to the main branch. Encourage developers to create feature branches and use pull requests for code changes.

Code Review Best Practices

Effective code reviews are crucial for identifying issues, sharing knowledge, and maintaining code quality. Here are some code review best practices:

Regular Reviews:

Conduct regular code reviews as part of your development process. Avoid delaying reviews until the end of a project.

Be Constructive:

Provide feedback in a constructive and respectful manner. Focus on the code and its quality, not on personal preferences.

Consistency:

Reviewers should ensure code consistency within the project. Check for consistent coding styles, naming conventions, and patterns.

Knowledge Sharing:

Code reviews are an opportunity to share knowledge and best practices. Encourage discussions and learning among team members.

Automated Checks:

Use automated code analysis tools and linters to catch common issues before they reach the code review stage.

Use Code Review Checklists:

Consider using code review checklists to ensure that important aspects, such as security, performance, and maintainability, are evaluated during reviews.

Conclusion

Pull requests and code reviews are integral to maintaining code quality, fostering collaboration, and catching issues early in the development process. By following best practices for creating and managing pull requests and conducting effective code reviews, teams can ensure that their codebase remains robust and reliable. Azure DevOps provides a comprehensive platform for implementing these practices, including built-in tools for code review and integration with continuous integration (CI) pipelines. In the following sections, we'll explore more advanced topics related to source control and project management within Azure DevOps.

3.5. Integrating with External Source Control Systems

While Azure DevOps provides its built-in version control systems, such as Git and Team Foundation Version Control (TFVC), there are scenarios where teams may need to integrate with external source control systems. This section explores the reasons for integrating with external systems and the approaches available within Azure DevOps.

Reasons for External Integration

Teams may have various reasons for integrating with external source control systems, including:

Legacy Systems:

Some organizations have existing source control systems that are deeply integrated into their development processes. Transitioning to a new system like Git can be challenging, so integration with the existing system is preferred.

Third-Party Dependencies:

Projects may depend on third-party libraries or components hosted in external repositories, such as GitHub or Bitbucket. Integrating with these systems allows teams to manage dependencies seamlessly.

Multi-Platform Development:

Teams working on cross-platform projects may need to access repositories hosted on different platforms. Integrating these repositories into a unified development workflow streamlines collaboration.

Integration Options

Azure DevOps offers several options for integrating with external source control systems:

Git Remote:

Azure DevOps can work with Git repositories hosted on external platforms by adding them as remotes. This allows developers to pull changes from and push changes to remote repositories seamlessly.

```
# Add a remote repository from GitHub

git remote add github-origin https://github.com/username/repo.git

# Pull changes from the external repository

git pull github-origin main

# Push changes to the external repository

git push github-origin main
```

Service Connections:

Azure DevOps provides service connections that allow teams to connect to external source control systems securely. These connections can be configured with credentials or tokens to access repositories on external platforms.

Webhooks and Triggers:

Webhooks and triggers in Azure DevOps can be used to automate actions when events occur in external repositories. For example, a webhook can trigger a build pipeline when changes are pushed to an external repository.

Mirror Repositories:

Azure DevOps supports mirroring repositories from external platforms. This means that changes made in the external repository are automatically mirrored in the Azure DevOps repository, keeping them in sync.

Azure Pipelines Integration:

Azure Pipelines, part of Azure DevOps, can be used to build and deploy code from external repositories. By configuring build and release pipelines, teams can automate the deployment process, even for code hosted externally.

Considerations for Integration

When integrating with external source control systems, teams should consider the following:

Authentication and Security:

Ensure that authentication mechanisms, such as tokens or credentials, are securely managed to access external repositories. Follow best practices for securing sensitive information.

Workflow and Automation:

Define workflows and automation rules for integrating external repositories with Azure DevOps. This includes setting up triggers, webhooks, and build pipelines to automate processes.

Monitoring and Sync:

Monitor the synchronization between the Azure DevOps repository and external repositories to detect any discrepancies or issues. Regularly check for updates and changes in external repositories.

Conclusion

Integrating with external source control systems is a practical solution for teams that need to collaborate with external partners, access third-party dependencies, or work with legacy systems. Azure DevOps offers various integration options, including Git remotes, service connections, webhooks, and mirroring repositories, to facilitate seamless collaboration with external repositories. By understanding the reasons for integration and following best practices, teams can ensure a smooth and secure development process, even when working with source control systems outside of Azure DevOps. In the following sections, we'll explore more aspects of Azure DevOps and its capabilities for software engineering and project management.

Chapter 4: Azure Pipelines - Continuous Integration and Deployment

4.1. Introduction to Azure Pipelines

Azure Pipelines is a robust and versatile platform for setting up continuous integration and continuous deployment (CI/CD) pipelines. It is a fundamental part of Azure DevOps, allowing teams to automate building, testing, and deploying applications. In this section, we'll introduce Azure Pipelines and its key concepts.

Understanding CI/CD

Continuous Integration (CI) and Continuous Deployment (CD) are software development practices that aim to automate and streamline the process of delivering software to production environments.

- **Continuous Integration (CI):** CI involves regularly integrating code changes from multiple contributors into a shared repository. With each integration, automated build and testing processes are triggered to identify and fix issues early.

- **Continuous Deployment (CD):** CD extends CI by automating the deployment of code to production or staging environments once it passes the CI pipeline. CD pipelines ensure that code changes are automatically and reliably delivered to end-users.

Key Concepts of Azure Pipelines

Azure Pipelines is designed to support various application types and languages. Here are some key concepts:

Pipelines:

A pipeline is a set of automated processes that define how your application is built, tested, and deployed. Pipelines are configured using YAML files, providing a version-controlled and reproducible definition of your CI/CD workflow.

Agents:

Agents are the execution environment for your pipelines. Azure DevOps provides hosted agents that are maintained by Microsoft, and you can also set up your own self-hosted agents for specific requirements.

Jobs:

A job is a set of steps that run on the same agent. Each job typically represents a stage in your CI/CD process, such as building the code, running tests, or deploying to a target environment.

Tasks:

Tasks are individual steps within a job. Azure Pipelines offers a wide range of built-in tasks for common operations like compiling code, running tests, and deploying to various platforms. You can also create custom tasks if needed.

Artifacts:

Artifacts are the output of a build pipeline, such as compiled binaries, libraries, or deployment packages. These artifacts can be published and used by subsequent stages or pipelines.

Benefits of Azure Pipelines

Azure Pipelines offers several benefits to development teams:

- **Automation:** Automate repetitive tasks like code compilation, testing, and deployment, reducing manual effort and minimizing the risk of human errors.

- **Consistency:** Ensure consistent build and deployment processes across different environments, leading to more reliable software releases.

- **Visibility:** Gain visibility into the status of your CI/CD pipelines with detailed logs and reports, making it easier to diagnose and resolve issues.

- **Scalability:** Azure Pipelines can scale to accommodate projects of various sizes and complexities, from small applications to large enterprise solutions.

- **Integration:** Integrate with a wide range of development tools and platforms, enabling a seamless workflow within your development ecosystem.

In the following sections, we'll delve deeper into creating and configuring pipelines, implementing CI, and setting up CD pipelines using Azure Pipelines.

4.2. Creating and Configuring Pipelines

Creating and configuring pipelines is a fundamental step in setting up continuous integration and continuous deployment (CI/CD) workflows in Azure DevOps using Azure Pipelines. In this section, we'll explore the process of creating and configuring pipelines, including key concepts and best practices.

Pipeline Creation

To create a pipeline in Azure Pipelines, follow these steps:

1. **Sign in to Azure DevOps:** Access your Azure DevOps organization and project.
2. **Navigate to Pipelines:** In the project's dashboard, click on "Pipelines" in the left navigation menu.
3. **Create a New Pipeline:**

– If this is your first pipeline, click "New Pipeline."

– If you have existing pipelines, click "New Pipeline" or "Create Pipeline."

1. **Select a Repository:** Choose the source code repository where your application's code is hosted. Azure Pipelines supports Git repositories, TFVC, and others.
2. **Configure the Pipeline:**

– Azure DevOps provides templates for various programming languages and frameworks. You can start with a template or create a pipeline from scratch.

– Configure the build and deployment steps in the pipeline using a YAML file or the visual designer.

1. **Save and Run:** Once the pipeline is configured, save it. You can also choose to run it manually or trigger it automatically upon code changes.

Key Concepts in Pipeline Configuration

YAML Configuration:

Pipelines in Azure DevOps are commonly defined using YAML (YAML Ain't Markup Language) syntax. YAML files describe the steps, jobs, and stages in your pipeline in a human-readable format. Here's a simple YAML example for a build pipeline:

trigger:

- main

pool:

vmImage: 'ubuntu-latest'

steps:

- script: echo Hello, World!

displayName: 'Run a one-line script'

Jobs and Stages:

Jobs represent units of work within a pipeline. They can run concurrently on different agents or sequentially, depending on the configuration. Stages group jobs together and define their execution order. Stages can represent build, test, deployment, or other phases in your pipeline.

Variables and Environment:

You can define variables and environments in your pipeline to parameterize and customize the pipeline's behavior. Variables can be used to store secrets and configuration settings securely.

Triggers:

Pipeline triggers determine when a pipeline should run. Common triggers include code commits, pull requests, and scheduled builds. You can configure triggers to automate your CI/CD workflow.

Pipeline Best Practices

When creating and configuring pipelines in Azure DevOps, consider the following best practices:

- **Version Control:** Store your pipeline configuration as code in your source code repository. This ensures versioning and reproducibility of your pipeline.

- **Modularity:** Keep pipelines modular by breaking them into smaller jobs and stages. This simplifies maintenance and allows for parallel execution.

- **Environment Isolation:** Use separate environments for different stages of your pipeline, such as development, staging, and production. This helps maintain consistent configurations.

- **Testing:** Incorporate automated tests into your pipeline to catch issues early in the development process. Test at each stage, from build to deployment.

- **Artifact Management:** Use Azure Pipelines to publish and manage build artifacts. These artifacts can be consumed in subsequent stages or pipelines.

- **Security:** Securely manage secrets and sensitive information using Azure DevOps secrets or variable groups. Avoid hardcoding secrets in your pipeline.

Conclusion

Creating and configuring pipelines in Azure Pipelines is a crucial step in implementing a CI/CD workflow for your applications. By defining pipelines as code using YAML and following best practices, you can ensure that your software development process is automated, consistent, and reliable. In the next sections, we'll explore more advanced topics related to continuous integration and deployment using Azure Pipelines.

4.3. Implementing Continuous Integration (CI)

Continuous Integration (CI) is a software development practice that involves regularly integrating code changes from multiple contributors into a shared repository. With each integration, automated build and testing processes are triggered to identify and fix issues early in the development process. In this section, we'll focus on implementing CI using Azure Pipelines.

Setting Up CI in Azure Pipelines

To implement CI in Azure Pipelines, follow these steps:

1. **Pipeline Configuration:** Create a pipeline configuration file (usually in YAML format) that defines the CI

workflow. This file specifies the steps to build, test, and validate your code. Here's a simplified example:

```
trigger:

- main

pool:

vmImage: 'ubuntu-latest'

steps:

- script: |

# Build your code

npm install

npm build

displayName: 'Build the project'

- script: |

# Run tests

npm test

displayName: 'Run tests'
```

1. **Integration with Source Control:** Ensure that your pipeline configuration file is stored in the same repository as your application code. This enables Azure Pipelines to detect changes in the repository and automatically trigger CI builds.
2. **Commit and Push Changes:** Commit your changes to the repository and push them to the remote repository

(e.g., GitHub, Azure Repos).

3. **Pipeline Execution:** Azure Pipelines detects the code changes and triggers the CI pipeline according to your defined configuration. It automatically provisions the necessary build agents and executes the CI tasks.

Key CI Practices

Implementing CI effectively involves following key practices:

Automated Testing:

CI pipelines should include automated tests that cover unit tests, integration tests, and any other relevant testing suites. Automated tests ensure that code changes don't introduce regressions.

Frequent Commits:

Encourage team members to commit and push their code changes frequently. Smaller, more frequent commits make it easier to detect and fix issues early.

Isolation of Builds:

Ensure that each CI build is isolated from other builds. Isolation prevents one build from affecting or being affected by another. Use clean environments for each build.

Parallel Execution:

Leverage parallel execution capabilities in your CI pipeline to speed up the build and test process. Azure Pipelines can run multiple jobs concurrently.

Artifact Publishing:

If your application produces build artifacts (e.g., binaries, packages), publish them as build artifacts or to a package feed for further use in deployment pipelines.

Notifications:

Set up notifications and alerts to inform team members of the CI build status. This helps teams stay informed and respond quickly to build failures.

Benefits of CI

Implementing CI offers several advantages to development teams:

- **Early Issue Detection:** CI helps catch integration issues, regressions, and bugs early in the development cycle, reducing the time and effort required to resolve them.

- **Consistency:** CI ensures that code is built, tested, and validated consistently across all development environments, leading to more reliable software.

- **Rapid Feedback:** Developers receive rapid feedback on their code changes, allowing them to iterate and make improvements quickly.

- **Automated Releases:** CI sets the foundation for Continuous Deployment (CD), enabling automatic and reliable software releases.

- **Improved Collaboration:** CI promotes collaboration among team members by encouraging frequent code integration and communication.

In conclusion, implementing Continuous Integration (CI) using Azure Pipelines is a crucial step toward building high-quality software. By automating build and test processes, detecting issues early, and following CI best practices, development teams can streamline their workflows and deliver more reliable software products. In the following sections, we'll explore Continuous Deployment (CD) and more advanced CI/CD topics.

4.4. Implementing Continuous Deployment (CD)

Continuous Deployment (CD) is the practice of automatically deploying code changes to production or staging environments after they have passed the Continuous Integration (CI) pipeline. CD aims to ensure that code is always in a deployable state and can be released to users quickly and reliably. In this section, we'll explore the implementation of CD using Azure Pipelines.

Key Concepts of Continuous Deployment

Continuous Deployment involves the following key concepts:

Deployment Environments:

Environments represent the target locations where your application will be deployed, such as development, staging, and production. Each environment typically mirrors a real-world deployment scenario.

Deployment Jobs:

A deployment job is a set of tasks that define how your application should be deployed to a specific environment. It includes tasks for deploying code, configuring resources, and running any necessary scripts.

Approvals and Gates:

CD pipelines often include approval and gating mechanisms to control the deployment process. Approvals can be manual or automated, and gates can enforce conditions before allowing a deployment to proceed.

Deployment Strategies:

CD pipelines can use various deployment strategies, including blue-green deployments, canary releases, and rolling deployments. These strategies control how new code is introduced to users while minimizing risks.

Implementing CD in Azure Pipelines

To implement Continuous Deployment in Azure Pipelines, follow these steps:

1. **Pipeline Configuration:** Create a CD pipeline configuration file (usually in YAML format) that defines the deployment workflow. This file specifies the environments, deployment jobs, and deployment strategies. Here's a simplified example:

```
trigger:
```

```
- main
pr:
- '*'
stages:
- stage: DeployToDev
jobs:
- job: Deploy
steps:
- script: |
# Deploy to the development environment
./deploy.sh dev
displayName: 'Deploy to Dev'
- stage: DeployToStaging
jobs:
- job: Deploy
steps:
- script: |
# Deploy to the staging environment
./deploy.sh staging
displayName: 'Deploy to Staging'
```

```
- stage: DeployToProduction
jobs:
- job: Deploy
steps:
- script: |
# Deploy to the production environment
./deploy.sh production
displayName: 'Deploy to Production'
```

1. **Integration with CI:** Ensure that your CD pipeline is triggered automatically after the CI pipeline successfully completes. Azure Pipelines can be configured to automatically trigger CD deployments upon successful CI builds.
2. **Deployment Jobs:** Define deployment jobs for each environment you want to deploy to. These jobs specify the steps required to deploy your application to the target environment.
3. **Approval and Gates:** Configure approvals and gates as needed for each deployment stage. This could include manual approvals or automated checks, such as automated testing or monitoring.
4. **Deployment Strategies:** Choose an appropriate deployment strategy based on your application's requirements. Azure Pipelines supports various strategies, allowing you to control the release of new code to users.

Benefits of CD

Implementing Continuous Deployment offers several advantages:

- **Rapid Releases:** CD enables rapid and automated releases of code changes to production, reducing time-to-market and delivering new features and bug fixes quickly.

- **Reduced Risk:** CD practices, such as canary releases and automated testing, help reduce the risk of introducing defects or regressions in production.

- **Consistency:** CD ensures that deployments are consistent across different environments, leading to more reliable and predictable deployments.

- **Automated Rollbacks:** In case of deployment issues, CD pipelines can be configured to automatically roll back to a previous, known-good state.

- **Improved Collaboration:** CD encourages collaboration between development, operations, and testing teams by automating the deployment process and reducing manual intervention.

In conclusion, implementing Continuous Deployment (CD) using Azure Pipelines is essential for delivering software quickly, reliably, and with reduced risk. By defining deployment workflows, using deployment strategies, and incorporating approval and gating mechanisms, development teams can automate the release process and achieve a higher level of software delivery efficiency. In the following sections, we'll explore advanced topics related to CI/CD and Azure Pipelines.

4.5. Advanced Pipeline Scenarios and Techniques

In Azure Pipelines, there are advanced scenarios and techniques that can enhance the flexibility and effectiveness of your Continuous Integration and Continuous Deployment (CI/CD) pipelines. These techniques enable you to handle complex workflows, manage resources efficiently, and optimize your CI/CD processes. In this section, we'll explore some of these advanced pipeline scenarios and techniques.

Multi-Stage Pipelines

Multi-stage pipelines allow you to define more complex CI/CD workflows with multiple stages, each representing a different phase of your deployment process. You can use multi-stage pipelines for scenarios like building, testing, deploying, and releasing software. Here's a simplified example:

```
trigger:
- main
stages:
- stage: Build
jobs:
- job: Build
steps:
- script: npm install
- script: npm build
```

```
- stage: Test

jobs:

- job: Test

steps:

- script: npm test

- stage: Deploy

jobs:

- job: DeployToStaging

steps:

- script: ./deploy.sh staging

- job: DeployToProduction

dependsOn: DeployToStaging

steps:

- script: ./deploy.sh production
```

In this example, the pipeline has three stages: Build, Test, and Deploy. Each stage consists of one or more jobs, and the deployment to the production environment depends on the successful completion of the staging deployment.

Matrix Builds

Matrix builds allow you to run a job or a set of jobs with multiple configurations, such as different versions of operating systems, programming languages, or dependencies. Matrix builds help ensure compatibility across different environments. Here's a simplified example:

```
jobs:

- job: BuildAndTest

strategy:

matrix:

os: [windows-latest, ubuntu-latest, macOS-latest]

node: [10.x, 12.x, 14.x]

steps:

- name: Set up Node.js ${{ matrix.node }}

uses: actions/setup-node@v2

with:

node-version: ${{ matrix.node }}

- name: Check out code

uses: actions/checkout@v2

- name: Install dependencies

run: npm install

- name: Build and test

run: npm build && npm test
```

In this example, the job "BuildAndTest" runs with different combinations of operating systems and Node.js versions, allowing you to test your application across various environments.

Agent Pools and Demands

Azure Pipelines provides agent pools that consist of groups of build and deployment agents. You can configure your pipelines to use specific agent pools or specify agent demands to run jobs on agents that meet specific criteria, such as having specific tools or capabilities. This allows you to optimize resource usage and ensure jobs are executed on suitable agents.

Self-Hosted Agents

Self-hosted agents are agents that you set up and manage in your own infrastructure. They can be used for specific scenarios where you need more control over the execution environment, such as accessing on-premises resources or specialized hardware. Azure Pipelines supports self-hosted agents that can be used alongside Microsoft-hosted agents.

Custom Tasks and Extensions

Azure Pipelines allows you to create custom tasks and extensions to extend the functionality of your pipelines. Custom tasks can be used to perform specific actions or integrate with third-party tools and services. You can develop custom tasks using various programming languages and frameworks.

Conditional Execution

You can use conditional expressions in your pipeline configuration to conditionally execute certain steps or jobs based on specific criteria. Conditional execution helps you handle dynamic scenarios and adapt your pipeline based on variables or outputs from previous steps.

These advanced pipeline scenarios and techniques provide you with the flexibility to create sophisticated CI/CD workflows that meet your organization's unique requirements. By understanding and leveraging these capabilities, you can optimize your Azure Pipelines to efficiently build, test, and deploy software while maintaining high-quality standards. In the next sections, we'll explore more aspects of Azure DevOps and its capabilities for software engineering and project management.

Chapter 5: Azure Test Plans - Testing Strategies

5.1. Introduction to Azure Test Plans

Azure Test Plans is a comprehensive testing tool offered as part of Azure DevOps Services, designed to help development teams plan, track, and manage their testing efforts effectively. It provides a set of features and tools that enable teams to design, execute, and report on test cases, ensuring the quality and reliability of their software applications.

Key Features of Azure Test Plans

Azure Test Plans offers a range of features to support various testing scenarios:

Test Case Management:

- **Test Case Creation:** Create and organize test cases, specifying steps, expected results, and associated requirements.

- **Test Case Iterations:** Define multiple iterations of a test case to cover different scenarios.

- **Test Case History:** Maintain a history of test case changes for auditing and tracking purposes.

Test Execution:

- **Manual Testing:** Execute test cases manually and record test results in a structured manner.
- **Exploratory Testing:** Perform exploratory testing sessions, capturing notes and screenshots.
- **Automated Testing:** Integrate automated test scripts and execute them as part of your testing process.

Test Plans and Suites:

- **Test Plans:** Organize test cases into test plans to manage testing efforts for specific milestones or releases.
- **Test Suites:** Create test suites to group related test cases, making it easier to execute tests in batches.

Traceability and Integration:

- **Requirements Traceability:** Link test cases to user stories, requirements, or other work items for traceability.
- **Azure DevOps Integration:** Seamlessly integrate with Azure DevOps work items, pipelines, and dashboards.

Reporting and Analytics:

- **Test Results:** View detailed test results, including pass/fail status, attachments, and historical data.

• **Test Analytics:** Analyze testing progress, trends, and quality metrics through interactive dashboards.

Test Planning and Design

In Azure Test Plans, the first step is to create a test plan and define the scope of your testing effort. This involves:

1. **Creating a Test Plan:** Start by creating a test plan that represents the testing effort for a specific milestone, release, or sprint.
2. **Defining Test Suites:** Inside a test plan, organize your test cases into test suites. Test suites are logical groupings of test cases based on criteria such as functionality, priority, or feature.
3. **Creating Test Cases:** Design and create individual test cases. Each test case should have a clear description, steps to reproduce, expected results, and any preconditions.
4. **Linking to Requirements:** Link your test cases to user stories, requirements, or other work items in Azure DevOps for traceability. This ensures that testing efforts align with project requirements.

Manual Testing

Azure Test Plans supports manual testing by allowing testers to execute test cases step by step and record test results. Manual testing involves the following steps:

1. **Selecting Test Cases:** Choose the test cases you want to execute from the test suite.
2. **Executing Test Cases:** Follow the steps outlined in the test cases, recording pass/fail results and adding comments or attachments as needed.

3. **Capturing Defects:** If a test case fails, capture and report defects with detailed information, including steps to reproduce and attachments.
4. **Exploratory Testing:** Conduct exploratory testing sessions where testers explore the application, capture notes, and take screenshots to report issues.

Automated Testing Integration

Azure Test Plans allows teams to integrate automated test scripts into their testing process. This includes:

1. **Test Automation Frameworks:** Implement test automation using popular frameworks like Selenium, Appium, or custom scripts.
2. **Test Execution:** Execute automated test scripts as part of your testing pipeline or manually trigger them within Azure Test Plans.
3. **Test Result Reporting:** View and analyze automated test results, including pass/fail status and test logs.

By integrating automated testing, teams can achieve faster and more consistent testing while reducing the manual effort required for regression testing.

Conclusion

Azure Test Plans is a powerful testing solution that empowers development teams to plan, execute, and track their testing efforts efficiently. With features for test case management, manual testing, automated testing integration, and robust reporting, Azure Test Plans enhances the quality of software applications and helps teams deliver reliable products to customers. In the following sections, we'll delve deeper into test case management, automation, and advanced testing strategies using Azure Test Plans.

5.2. Designing and Managing Test Cases

In the realm of software testing, designing and managing test cases is a fundamental aspect of ensuring the quality and reliability of your applications. Azure Test Plans provides a robust set of tools and features to help development teams create, organize, and manage test cases effectively.

Test Case Design Best Practices

When designing test cases in Azure Test Plans, it's essential to follow best practices to create comprehensive and effective test coverage. Here are some key principles to keep in mind:

Clarity and Precision:

- **Clear and Concise Steps:** Write test case steps in a clear and concise manner. Each step should be easy to understand and follow.

- **Expected Results:** Clearly define the expected results for each step. Testers should know what outcome to expect.

Test Case Reusability:

- **Modular Test Cases:** Design test cases in a modular fashion. Create reusable test steps that can be used across multiple test cases.

- **Parameterization:** Use parameterization to create data-driven test cases. This allows you to test various scenarios with different input data.

Coverage and Traceability:

- **Link to Requirements:** Ensure that test cases are linked to relevant requirements, user stories, or other work items in Azure DevOps for traceability.

- **Coverage Matrix:** Maintain a coverage matrix to track which requirements or features are covered by which test cases.

Maintainability:

- **Regular Updates:** Keep test cases up to date as the application evolves. Updates may be needed due to changes in requirements or application functionality.

- **Versioning:** Consider versioning test cases to track changes and historical data.

Creating Test Cases

Azure Test Plans provides a user-friendly interface for creating test cases. Here's an overview of the steps involved:

1. **Navigate to Test Plans:** Access the Test Plans module within Azure DevOps.
2. **Select a Test Plan:** Choose the test plan you want to work with, or create a new one.
3. **Create Test Suite:** Inside the test plan, create a test suite to

organize your test cases. Test suites are typically used to group related test cases, such as those for a specific feature or functionality.

4. **Add Test Case:** Within a test suite, click to add a new test case. Provide a title, description, and other relevant information.
5. **Define Steps:** In the test case, define the steps required to execute the test. For each step, specify the action and expected result.
6. **Parameterization (Optional):** If needed, parameterize your test case to enable data-driven testing. Parameters can be linked to test data tables.
7. **Link to Work Items:** Link the test case to related work items, such as user stories or requirements, for traceability.
8. **Save and Update:** Save the test case, and continue creating additional test cases as needed.

Organizing Test Cases

As your test suite grows, it's crucial to maintain an organized structure for your test cases. Azure Test Plans offers features to help you organize and manage your test cases efficiently:

Test Suites:

- **Create Multiple Suites:** Create multiple test suites within a test plan to group test cases logically.

- **Test Suite Hierarchy:** Build a hierarchy of test suites to represent different levels of testing (e.g., feature-level, regression-level).

Test Case Filters:

- **Test Case Queries:** Utilize test case queries to filter and display specific test cases based on criteria like priority, area, or state.

- **Shared Queries:** Share test case queries with team members for consistency.

Tags and Labels:

- **Tags:** Apply tags to test cases to categorize and label them. Tags help in quick identification and filtering.

- **Custom Fields:** Create custom fields to capture additional metadata specific to your testing process.

Test Case Maintenance

Test case maintenance is an ongoing process to ensure that your test cases remain relevant and effective. Here are some practices for test case maintenance:

- **Regular Review:** Periodically review and update test cases to reflect changes in application functionality or requirements.

- **Retirement:** Consider retiring test cases that are no longer relevant or applicable.

- **Version Control:** Implement version control for test cases to track changes and historical data.

- **Traceability:** Ensure that test cases remain linked to relevant work items to maintain traceability.

- **Reusability:** Identify opportunities for reusing test cases or test steps across different test suites or test plans.

In conclusion, designing and managing test cases is a critical component of a successful testing strategy. Azure Test Plans provides a robust platform to create, organize, and maintain test cases effectively. By following best practices for test case design, organization, and maintenance, development teams can ensure thorough testing and reliable software quality. In the following sections, we'll explore automated testing, integration with Azure DevOps, and advanced testing strategies using Azure Test Plans.

5.3. Automated Testing in Azure DevOps

Automated testing is a crucial component of modern software development and testing practices. It allows development teams to execute test cases automatically, ensuring that code changes do not introduce regressions and that the software remains in a reliable state throughout its lifecycle. Azure DevOps provides robust support for automated testing through various tools and integrations, enabling teams to automate unit tests, integration tests, and more.

Key Benefits of Automated Testing

Automated testing offers several benefits to development teams:

Faster Feedback:

Automated tests can be executed quickly, providing immediate feedback to developers about the impact of their code changes. This rapid feedback loop accelerates the development process.

Consistency:

Automated tests are executed in a consistent and reproducible manner. This consistency helps identify and address issues early in the development cycle.

Regression Testing:

Automated tests are ideal for regression testing, ensuring that new code changes do not introduce defects or break existing functionality.

Increased Test Coverage:

With automation, it becomes feasible to achieve higher test coverage, including edge cases and scenarios that may be time-consuming to test manually.

Continuous Integration (CI) and Continuous Deployment (CD) Integration:

Automated tests can be seamlessly integrated into CI/CD pipelines, allowing for automatic testing of code changes and ensuring that only reliable code is deployed to production.

Types of Automated Tests

Azure DevOps supports various types of automated tests, including:

Unit Tests:

Unit tests focus on testing individual components or functions of an application in isolation. They are typically written by developers to validate the correctness of small code units.

Integration Tests:

Integration tests verify the interactions and integrations between different components or modules of an application. They ensure that various parts of the system work together as expected.

UI Tests:

UI tests, also known as end-to-end tests or acceptance tests, validate the behavior of an application from a user's perspective. These tests interact with the application's user interface to simulate user actions and check for expected outcomes.

Performance Tests:

Performance tests assess the responsiveness and scalability of an application under different load conditions. Azure DevOps can integrate with performance testing tools to automate this process.

Security Tests:

Security tests assess the security posture of an application by identifying vulnerabilities and potential security risks. Automated security testing tools can be integrated into the pipeline.

Implementing Automated Tests in Azure DevOps

To implement automated tests in Azure DevOps, follow these general steps:

1. **Choose Testing Frameworks:** Select the testing frameworks and tools that align with your project's technology stack. Popular choices include NUnit, xUnit, MSTest for unit tests, and tools like Selenium for UI testing.
2. **Write Test Scripts:** Develop test scripts or test cases that cover different aspects of your application. Ensure that these scripts are automated and can be executed by the chosen testing frameworks.
3. **Create Test Projects:** Organize your test scripts into test projects within your source code repository. Ensure that these test projects are part of your DevOps pipeline.
4. **Configure CI/CD Pipelines:** Set up CI/CD pipelines that include steps for building, testing, and deploying your application. Configure the pipeline to trigger automated tests as part of the build and deployment process.
5. **Integrate with Azure DevOps:** Azure DevOps integrates seamlessly with popular testing frameworks and tools. You can leverage Azure DevOps' capabilities to schedule and execute automated tests.
6. **Test Execution and Reporting:** Automated tests are executed as part of your CI/CD pipeline. The results are

reported back to Azure DevOps, allowing you to track test execution, pass/fail status, and any defects found.

Test Automation Best Practices

To maximize the benefits of automated testing in Azure DevOps, consider the following best practices:

- **Test Early and Often:** Integrate automated tests into your CI/CD pipeline to test code changes as soon as they are committed.

- **Parallel Testing:** Utilize parallel testing to distribute test execution across multiple agents, reducing test execution time.

- **Environment Isolation:** Ensure that tests are executed in isolated environments to prevent interference between test runs.

- **Test Data Management:** Manage test data effectively, including data setup, teardown, and test data variations.

- **Continuous Test Maintenance:** Regularly update and maintain automated tests to keep them aligned with changes in the application.

- **Reporting and Monitoring:** Leverage Azure DevOps' reporting and monitoring capabilities to track test results and identify trends.

- **Code Quality and Test Coverage:** Integrate code quality checks and code coverage analysis into your CI/CD pipeline to maintain code quality standards.

In conclusion, automated testing is a vital practice for ensuring software quality and reliability in modern software development. Azure DevOps provides a comprehensive platform for implementing and managing automated tests across various testing types. By automating tests and integrating them into your CI/CD pipelines, development teams can deliver high-quality software more efficiently and with greater confidence.

5.4. Integrating Testing into CI/CD Pipelines

The integration of testing into Continuous Integration and Continuous Deployment (CI/CD) pipelines is a critical step in ensuring the quality and reliability of software applications. Azure DevOps provides robust capabilities for seamlessly incorporating various types of tests into your CI/CD workflows, enabling automated testing at every stage of the software development lifecycle.

Key Benefits of CI/CD Integration

Integrating testing into CI/CD pipelines offers several advantages:

Early Detection of Issues:

By running tests automatically on every code commit, you can identify and address issues at an early stage, reducing the cost and effort of fixing defects later in the development cycle.

Consistency and Reproducibility:

CI/CD pipelines execute tests consistently and reproducibly, ensuring that tests are performed under controlled conditions and yielding reliable results.

Faster Feedback:

Automated tests in CI/CD pipelines provide rapid feedback to developers, allowing them to address problems quickly and maintain a high pace of development.

Reliable Deployments:

Testing in CI/CD pipelines ensures that only code that passes all tests is deployed to production, minimizing the risk of deploying defective software.

Types of Testing in CI/CD Pipelines

Azure DevOps supports the integration of various types of tests into CI/CD pipelines, including:

Unit Testing:

Unit tests are typically executed in the build stage of a CI/CD pipeline. These tests validate the correctness of individual code units, such as functions or classes. Popular unit testing frameworks like NUnit, xUnit, and MSTest can be integrated with Azure DevOps pipelines.

Integration Testing:

Integration tests verify the interactions between different components or services within an application. They are executed in the CI/CD pipeline to ensure that integrated parts of the application function correctly together.

UI Testing:

UI tests, also known as end-to-end tests, simulate user interactions with the application's user interface. Tools like Selenium and Puppeteer can be integrated into CI/CD pipelines to automate UI testing.

Performance Testing:

Performance tests assess the application's responsiveness and scalability under different loads. Azure DevOps allows integration with performance testing tools to automate performance testing within pipelines.

Security Testing:

Security tests identify vulnerabilities and security risks in the application. These tests can be automated and integrated into CI/CD pipelines to ensure that security checks are performed before deployment.

Implementing Testing in CI/CD Pipelines

To integrate testing into CI/CD pipelines in Azure DevOps, follow these general steps:

1. **Define Test Stages:** Identify the appropriate stages in your CI/CD pipeline where testing should occur. Common stages include build, deployment to a staging environment, and deployment to production.
2. **Select Testing Tools:** Choose the testing frameworks and tools that align with the types of tests you want to run. Install and configure these tools within your CI/CD

pipeline agents.

3. **Configure Build and Release Pipelines:** In Azure DevOps, create or configure your build and release pipelines to include testing tasks or steps. Define which tests should run at each stage.
4. **Trigger Tests Automatically:** Set up triggers to automatically execute tests when code changes are committed, builds are triggered, or releases are deployed.
5. **Collect and Report Results:** Configure your pipeline to collect test results and report them back to Azure DevOps. This allows you to track test execution, pass/fail status, and any defects discovered.
6. **Failure Handling:** Implement appropriate failure handling mechanisms, such as failing the build or preventing deployment, when tests fail to ensure that only reliable code is promoted.

Test Environments and Infrastructure as Code (IaC)

To ensure consistency in testing, consider using Infrastructure as Code (IaC) principles to manage your test environments. Tools like Azure Resource Manager (ARM) templates or Terraform can be employed to automate the provisioning and configuration of test environments. By defining infrastructure as code, you can recreate identical test environments for each test run, reducing environmental variability.

Parallel Testing and Scaling

As your testing suite grows, it may be necessary to run tests in parallel to reduce test execution time. Azure DevOps allows you to scale your testing infrastructure by distributing tests across multiple agents, enabling faster feedback without overloading individual agents.

Conclusion

Integrating testing into CI/CD pipelines is a fundamental practice in modern software development. Azure DevOps offers a comprehensive platform for automating and managing various types of tests at every stage of the CI/CD process. By seamlessly incorporating testing into your pipelines, development teams can achieve early issue detection, maintain code quality, and ensure the reliable delivery of software to end-users. In the subsequent sections, we will explore advanced pipeline scenarios and techniques, as well as best practices for effective testing in Azure DevOps.

5.5. Tracking and Analyzing Test Results

Tracking and analyzing test results are essential aspects of any testing strategy within Azure DevOps. By systematically capturing and evaluating test outcomes, development teams can gain valuable insights into the quality of their software and make informed decisions for improvement.

The Importance of Test Result Analysis

Effective test result analysis provides numerous benefits:

Defect Identification:

Analyzing test results helps identify defects, inconsistencies, and issues in the software under test. These findings can then be addressed promptly.

Quality Assessment:

Test result analysis offers a quantifiable measure of software quality. It helps gauge the reliability, functionality, and performance of the application.

Continuous Improvement:

By tracking test results over time, development teams can identify trends and patterns, leading to continuous improvement in processes and code quality.

Decision-Making:

Test results aid decision-making during release planning, helping determine whether the software is ready for deployment or requires further refinement.

Tracking Test Results in Azure DevOps

Azure DevOps provides features for tracking and managing test results effectively:

Test Runs and Test Suites:

Azure DevOps allows you to organize test cases into test suites and execute them as test runs. Each test run generates detailed results that can be reviewed and analyzed.

Test Outcome History:

The history of test outcomes is stored in Azure DevOps, enabling you to compare current and historical results to identify changes in software quality.

Work Item Integration:

Linking test cases to work items (e.g., user stories, bugs) in Azure DevOps facilitates traceability between requirements and test execution. You can easily view the status of associated work items based on test results.

Attachments and Logs:

Test results often include attachments and logs, providing additional context for test failures. These attachments can be reviewed within Azure DevOps.

Analyzing Test Results

Analyzing test results involves reviewing test outcome data, identifying patterns, and making informed decisions. Key steps in test result analysis include:

Pass/Fail Analysis:

Categorize test cases as pass or fail based on their outcomes. Identify the reasons for failures and prioritize defects for resolution.

Trend Analysis:

Track test results over time to identify trends. A sudden increase in failures or consistent pass rates can indicate areas of concern.

Test Case Status:

Review the status of individual test cases. Determine whether any critical test cases have failed, as these may block further development or release.

Failure Root Cause:

Investigate the root causes of test failures. Was it a code issue, a test data problem, or an environment-related problem? Address the root causes accordingly.

Code Coverage Analysis:

Analyze code coverage data to determine how much of your codebase is exercised by tests. Identify areas with low code coverage and consider adding additional tests.

Test Execution Time:

Evaluate the time taken for test execution. Long-running tests may impact pipeline efficiency, and optimizing test execution time can lead to faster feedback.

Reporting and Visualization

Azure DevOps offers reporting and visualization tools to help teams make sense of test result datá:

Dashboards:

Create customized dashboards that display key testing metrics, such as pass/fail rates, test execution trends, and code coverage percentages.

Queries and Charts:

Azure DevOps allows you to create queries and charts to visualize test data. Queries can filter and display specific test cases or work items based on criteria.

Azure Test Plans:

Leverage the reporting and analytics capabilities within Azure Test Plans to access detailed insights into test results, test case coverage, and execution history.

Continuous Improvement

The insights gained from test result analysis should drive continuous improvement efforts. Development teams should use this information to refine testing strategies, enhance test coverage, and prioritize bug fixes. Continuous improvement is a fundamental aspect of maintaining software quality and delivering reliable applications to end-users.

In conclusion, tracking and analyzing test results are integral parts of the software testing process in Azure DevOps. These practices enable development teams to detect defects, assess software quality, and make data-driven decisions. By consistently reviewing test results, teams can drive continuous improvement and deliver higher-quality software to their customers. In the upcoming sections, we will explore other aspects of Azure DevOps, including package management, collaboration, and infrastructure as code (IaC).

Chapter 6: Azure Artifacts - Package Management

Chapter 6: Azure Artifacts - Package Management

6.1. Understanding Azure Artifacts

Azure Artifacts is a package management service provided by Microsoft Azure that simplifies the management of software packages used in your projects. Whether you are developing applications in .NET, Java, Node.js, Python, or any other language, Azure Artifacts enables you to efficiently store, publish, and consume packages within your development pipelines. This section delves into the fundamentals of Azure Artifacts and its significance in modern software development.

What Are Packages?

In the context of software development, packages are collections of reusable code, libraries, or dependencies that can be easily integrated into your projects. They enhance productivity by allowing developers to leverage existing solutions instead of reinventing the wheel. Packages can include libraries, frameworks, runtime components, and other assets necessary for building software.

The Role of Package Management

Package management is the practice of systematically organizing, storing, and distributing packages in a consistent and reliable manner. Effective package management offers several benefits, including:

- **Dependency Management:** Packages define dependencies on other packages, ensuring that the correct versions are used, reducing compatibility issues.

• **Version Control:** Packages are versioned, allowing you to specify the exact version of a package your project requires.

• **Reproducibility:** By referencing specific package versions, you can ensure that your project can be built consistently over time.

• **Security:** Package management systems often include security features, such as vulnerability scanning, to help identify and mitigate security risks.

• **Efficiency:** Package management streamlines the development process, as developers don't need to manually download and manage dependencies.

Azure Artifacts Overview

Azure Artifacts simplifies the process of managing and sharing packages in a development environment. It offers the following key features:

Package Feeds:

Package feeds are containers for organizing and storing packages. Azure Artifacts allows you to create multiple feeds to organize packages based on projects, teams, or purposes.

Package Types:

Azure Artifacts supports various package types, including NuGet, npm, Maven, and Python packages. This flexibility enables you to work with packages in your preferred language or ecosystem.

Secure Access Control:

Access to package feeds can be controlled through Azure DevOps permissions, ensuring that only authorized individuals or teams can publish or consume packages.

Integration with Azure DevOps:

Azure Artifacts seamlessly integrates with Azure DevOps, making it easy to include packages in your build and release pipelines.

Compatibility with External Sources:

You can configure Azure Artifacts to proxy and cache packages from external sources, reducing download times and ensuring availability.

Versioning and Lifecycle Management:

Azure Artifacts supports versioning, allowing you to manage different versions of your packages. Additionally, you can set retention policies for package versions to control storage costs.

Universal Packages:

Universal packages in Azure Artifacts provide a versatile solution for packaging and distributing any type of content, making it suitable for scenarios beyond code libraries.

Use Cases for Azure Artifacts

Azure Artifacts can benefit a wide range of development scenarios, including:

- **Enterprise Application Development:** Large organizations with multiple development teams can use Azure Artifacts to manage and share packages across projects.

- **Open-Source Projects:** Open-source maintainers can publish their libraries and packages to Azure Artifacts, making them easily accessible to the community.

- **Continuous Integration/Continuous Deployment (CI/CD):** Azure Artifacts integrates seamlessly with Azure DevOps pipelines, enabling automated package management in CI/CD workflows.

- **Private Package Sharing:** Teams can create private feeds to share proprietary packages within their organization securely.

In summary, Azure Artifacts simplifies package management, enabling teams to efficiently store, publish, and consume packages. It enhances collaboration, streamlines development workflows, and ensures the reliability of package dependencies in your projects. In the following sections, we will explore various aspects of using Azure Artifacts, including package management best practices and integration with CI/CD pipelines.

6.2. Managing NuGet, NPM, and Maven Packages

Azure Artifacts supports various package types, including NuGet, npm, and Maven packages. These package types cater to different ecosystems and programming languages, allowing you to manage dependencies and packages specific to your project's requirements.

In this section, we will explore how Azure Artifacts facilitates the management of these package types.

NuGet Packages

NuGet is a popular package manager for .NET development, and Azure Artifacts seamlessly integrates with it. Here's how you can manage NuGet packages using Azure Artifacts:

1. **Create a NuGet Feed:** To start managing NuGet packages, create a NuGet feed within Azure Artifacts. This feed will serve as the container for your NuGet packages.
2. **Publishing Packages:** You can publish NuGet packages to your feed either manually or through automated build pipelines. By pushing packages to the feed, you make them available to your development teams.
3. **Package Versions:** Azure Artifacts supports versioning of NuGet packages, allowing you to maintain multiple versions of the same package.
4. **Access Control:** Control who can publish and consume packages from your NuGet feed by configuring access permissions.
5. **Integration with Visual Studio:** Developers can easily configure Visual Studio to consume packages from your Azure Artifacts NuGet feed, simplifying the development process.

npm Packages

For JavaScript and Node.js development, npm is the package manager of choice. Azure Artifacts offers robust support for npm packages:

1. **Create an npm Feed:** Similar to NuGet, you can create an

npm feed in Azure Artifacts to host your npm packages.

2. **Publishing Packages:** Publish npm packages to your feed, making them accessible to your development teams. Azure DevOps pipelines can automate this process.
3. **Scoped Packages:** Azure Artifacts allows you to publish npm packages with scopes, helping organize and differentiate packages within your organization.
4. **Proxying Public npm Registry:** Azure Artifacts can be configured to proxy the public npm registry, ensuring faster downloads and reliability of packages.
5. **Integration with Package Managers:** Developers can configure their npm clients to use your Azure Artifacts feed as a registry source, enabling seamless package installation.

Maven Packages

For Java projects, Maven is a widely used build and dependency management tool. Azure Artifacts provides support for managing Maven packages:

1. **Create a Maven Feed:** Set up a Maven feed in Azure Artifacts, which will act as the repository for your Maven packages.
2. **Publishing Artifacts:** Publish your Maven artifacts to the feed, including JAR files, POM files, and other associated resources.
3. **Dependency Resolution:** Developers can include dependencies from your Azure Artifacts Maven feed in their Maven projects by configuring the settings.xml file.
4. **Versioning and Lifecycle:** Azure Artifacts allows you to version and manage Maven artifacts, ensuring that you can control and update dependencies.

5. **Access Control:** Implement access control policies to restrict who can publish and retrieve Maven packages from your feed.

By supporting these package types, Azure Artifacts offers a versatile solution for managing dependencies across different programming languages and ecosystems. Whether you're developing .NET applications, JavaScript libraries, or Java projects, Azure Artifacts simplifies the process of packaging, publishing, and consuming dependencies, leading to more efficient and reliable software development workflows. In the subsequent sections, we will explore further capabilities of Azure Artifacts, including integration with CI/CD pipelines and best practices for package management.

6.3. Integrating Package Management into CI/CD

Integrating package management into your Continuous Integration and Continuous Deployment (CI/CD) pipelines is crucial for maintaining a streamlined and automated software development process. Azure Artifacts seamlessly integrates with Azure DevOps pipelines, allowing you to automate package-related tasks as part of your CI/CD workflows. In this section, we will explore how to incorporate package management into your CI/CD pipelines using Azure Artifacts.

NuGet Package Integration

Publishing NuGet Packages

1. **Automated Publishing:** In your Azure DevOps YAML pipeline, you can add a step to publish NuGet packages to your Azure Artifacts NuGet feed. Use the

NuGetCommand@2 task with the push command to achieve this. Here's an example YAML snippet:

```
- task: NuGetCommand@2

inputs:

command: 'push'

packagesToPush:
'$(Build.ArtifactStagingDirectory)/*.nupkg'

nuGetFeedType: 'internal'

publishVstsFeed: '<YourFeedName>'

versioningScheme: 'off'
```

1. **Access Control:** Ensure that the pipeline has the necessary permissions to publish packages to the NuGet feed. You can manage permissions within Azure DevOps.

Consuming NuGet Packages

1. **Package Restore:** In your build pipeline, configure the NuGet Restore task to restore packages from your Azure Artifacts NuGet feed. Use the NuGetCommand@2 task with the restore command.

```
- task: NuGetCommand@2

inputs:

command: 'restore'

restoreSolution: '**/*.sln'
```

feedsToUse: 'select'

vstsFeed: '<YourFeedName>'

1. **Build and Deployment:** Once packages are restored, proceed with your build and deployment steps as usual.

npm Package Integration

Publishing npm Packages

1. **Automated Publishing:** In your Azure DevOps YAML pipeline, use the npmAuthenticate task to authenticate with your Azure Artifacts npm feed, and then use the npm publish command to publish npm packages.

- task: npmAuthenticate@0

- script: npm publish—registry https://pkgs.dev.azure.com/<YourOrganization>/_packaging/<Yo
registry/

1. **Access Control:** Ensure that the pipeline has the necessary permissions to publish packages to the npm feed. You can manage permissions within Azure DevOps.

Consuming npm Packages

1. **Package Installation:** In your build pipeline, configure the npm task to install packages from your Azure Artifacts npm feed. Set the registry URL to your feed's registry URL.

- script: npm install—registry https://pkgs.dev.azure.com/<YourOrganization>/_packaging/<You registry/

1. **Build and Deployment:** Proceed with your build and deployment steps once packages are installed.

Maven Package Integration

Publishing Maven Artifacts

1. **Automated Publishing:** In your Azure DevOps YAML pipeline, you can use the MavenAuthenticate task to authenticate with your Azure Artifacts Maven feed. Then, use the Maven task to publish Maven artifacts.

- task: MavenAuthenticate@0

- script: mvn deploy -DskipTests=true—settings ./path/to/settings.xml

1. **Access Control:** Ensure that the pipeline has the necessary permissions to publish artifacts to the Maven feed. Manage permissions within Azure DevOps.

Consuming Maven Artifacts

1. **Dependency Resolution:** Configure the settings.xml file in your build pipeline to include your Azure Artifacts Maven feed as a repository. Developers can then specify dependencies in their pom.xml files.

<repositories>

<repository>

<id>azure-artifacts**</id>**

<url>https://pkgs.dev.azure.com/**<YourOrganization>**/_packaging
v1**</url>**

</repository>

</repositories>

1. **Build and Deployment:** Continue with your Maven build and deployment steps once dependencies are resolved.

By integrating package management into your CI/CD pipelines with Azure Artifacts, you ensure that your applications are consistently built, tested, and deployed with the correct package versions and dependencies. This automation reduces manual intervention, streamlines workflows, and enhances the reliability of your software delivery process. In the following sections, we will delve deeper into best practices for package management and explore version control and dependency management using Azure Artifacts.

6.4. Version Control and Dependency Management

Version control and dependency management are critical aspects of package management within the context of Azure Artifacts. Ensuring that your projects use the correct versions of packages and dependencies is essential for maintaining the stability and reliability of your software. In this section, we will explore best practices for version control and dependency management with Azure Artifacts.

Version Control Best Practices

1. **Semantic Versioning (SemVer):** Adhere to the Semantic Versioning standard for your packages. SemVer consists of three numbers, Major.Minor.Patch, where each number has a specific meaning. Increment the Major version for backward-incompatible changes, the Minor version for backward-compatible new features, and the Patch version for backward-compatible bug fixes.
2. **Version Pinning:** Pin dependencies to specific versions in your project files (e.g., package.json for npm, pom.xml for Maven). Avoid using wildcards or range expressions that can lead to unexpected updates. Instead, explicitly specify the desired version.

```
// Example for npm package.json

"dependencies": {

"package-name": "1.2.3"

}
```

1. **Lock Files:** Utilize lock files or manifests (e.g., package-lock.json for npm, yarn.lock for Yarn) to ensure that the exact versions of packages are used across development and deployment environments.

Dependency Management Best Practices

1. **Private Feeds:** Consider using private feeds in Azure Artifacts for packages that are specific to your organization. This provides control over who can access and publish packages.

2. **Scoped Packages:** Use scoped packages to group related packages under a common namespace. Scoped packages make it easier to manage and publish related packages.
3. **Package Promotion:** Implement a promotion workflow where packages go through different stages (e.g., development, testing, production) before being widely used. Azure Artifacts allows you to promote packages between feeds.
4. **Dependency Auditing:** Regularly audit and review your project's dependencies to identify security vulnerabilities or outdated packages. Azure DevOps provides vulnerability scanning and alerts for packages.
5. **Automated Dependency Updates:** Consider using tools like Dependabot to automate the process of identifying and updating outdated dependencies in your projects.
6. **Dependency Analysis:** Leverage Azure Artifacts reports and analytics to gain insights into the usage of packages across your organization. This can help in making informed decisions about package retention and deprecation.
7. **Documentation:** Maintain clear and up-to-date documentation that includes information about package usage, versioning policies, and procedures for adding or updating dependencies.

Package Retention Policies

Establish package retention policies to manage the lifecycle of packages in your Azure Artifacts feeds. These policies define how long packages are retained and when they can be deleted. Consider factors such as compliance requirements, storage costs, and the need to keep historical versions for reference.

Package Deletion and Archiving

Azure Artifacts provides the ability to delete or archive packages when they are no longer needed. Deleting packages permanently removes them, while archiving preserves packages but makes them read-only. Implement a clear process for when and how packages are deleted or archived to avoid unintended data loss.

By following these best practices for version control and dependency management, you can ensure that your software projects are well-maintained, secure, and efficient. Azure Artifacts offers a robust platform for managing packages, enabling you to streamline your development workflows and deliver high-quality software consistently. In the next section, we will delve into best practices for collaboration and communication within Azure DevOps.

6.5. Best Practices for Azure Artifacts

In this section, we will explore best practices for using Azure Artifacts effectively. Azure Artifacts is a package management service that allows you to create, host, and share packages within your organization. These packages can include libraries, frameworks, and other components that your software projects depend on.

1. Organize Your Feeds

One of the first steps in using Azure Artifacts is to organize your feeds. Feeds are containers for your packages, and it's essential to structure them logically. Consider creating separate feeds for different types of packages, such as libraries, tools, or third-party dependencies. This organization simplifies access control and management.

2. Implement Access Control

Control access to your feeds by defining permissions and roles. Use Azure DevOps groups to manage who can view, publish, or delete packages within a feed. This ensures that only authorized team members can make changes to your packages, reducing the risk of accidental deletions or unauthorized access.

3. Use Universal Packages

Azure Artifacts supports various package formats, including NuGet, npm, Maven, and more. Consider using Universal Packages for scenarios where you need to package and distribute non-standard content, such as build outputs, scripts, or configuration files. Universal Packages provide flexibility and consistency across different types of content.

4. Package Versioning

Implement a clear versioning strategy for your packages. Use semantic versioning (SemVer) to indicate changes in your packages' compatibility. Ensure that package versions are intuitive, making it easy for consumers to understand the impact of updating to a new version.

5. Package Signing

For added security and trust, consider signing your packages with a digital signature. Package signing ensures that packages have not been tampered with and come from a trusted source. Azure Artifacts supports package signing for various package types, including NuGet and npm.

6. Package Retention Policies

Define package retention policies to manage the lifecycle of packages. Determine how long packages should be retained in your feeds before they are deleted or archived. Be mindful of compliance requirements and storage costs when setting retention policies.

7. Continuous Integration (CI) Integration

Integrate Azure Artifacts with your CI/CD pipelines to automate package publishing. When a build is successful, publish the generated packages to Azure Artifacts. This ensures that the latest packages are readily available for consumption by your development teams.

8. Dependency Scanning

Regularly scan your packages for known vulnerabilities and security issues. Azure Artifacts provides vulnerability scanning capabilities, helping you identify and address potential security risks in your dependencies.

9. Package Promotion Workflow

Implement a package promotion workflow to ensure that packages go through stages before being widely adopted. Stages may include development, testing, and production feeds. Promoting packages from one stage to another should involve testing and validation.

10. Documentation

Maintain comprehensive documentation for your packages, including usage instructions, version history, and any required configuration. Documentation helps consumers of your packages understand how to use them effectively.

11. Monitoring and Analytics

Leverage Azure Artifacts' monitoring and analytics features to gain insights into package usage. Monitoring helps you track the popularity of packages, while analytics can inform decisions about package retention and deprecation.

By following these best practices, you can maximize the benefits of Azure Artifacts in your organization. Azure Artifacts simplifies package management, enhances security, and improves collaboration among development teams. Properly managed packages contribute to the overall stability and reliability of your software projects.

7.1. Effective Team Collaboration using Azure DevOps

Effective team collaboration is the cornerstone of successful software development projects. Azure DevOps provides a robust set of tools and features to support collaboration among team members, regardless of their geographical locations. In this section, we will explore best practices for fostering collaboration within your development teams using Azure DevOps.

1. Project Setup and Organization

- Begin by setting up your projects and repositories in Azure DevOps in a well-organized manner. Use logical project and repository names that reflect their purpose.

- Consider creating separate projects for different product lines or teams to maintain separation and clarity.

2. Work Item Tracking with Azure Boards

- Utilize Azure Boards to manage work items, user stories, tasks, and bugs. Create and assign work items to team members, allowing for clear accountability.

- Use customizable Kanban boards or Scrum boards to visualize and manage work in progress.

3. Integration with Microsoft Teams and Communication Tools

- Integrate Azure DevOps with Microsoft Teams or other communication tools used by your team. This integration enables real-time communication and updates.

- Set up notifications to alert team members about work item changes, build statuses, and other important events directly within their communication platform.

4. Managing Permissions and Access Control

- Define permissions and access control policies to ensure that team members have appropriate access to resources.

- Regularly review and update permissions to align with changing team dynamics and project requirements.

5. Utilizing Dashboards and Reporting

- Create customized dashboards in Azure DevOps to provide real-time visibility into project progress and key metrics.

- Use reports and analytics to gain insights into team performance, sprint progress, and release planning.

6. Branching and Code Review

- Implement branching strategies that suit your development workflow. Common strategies include feature branching, release branching, and Gitflow.

• Enforce code review practices by requiring pull requests before code is merged. Use Azure Repos pull request features to facilitate code reviews and discussions.

7. Automated Testing and CI/CD Integration

• Integrate Azure DevOps with your continuous integration/continuous deployment (CI/CD) pipelines. This ensures that code changes are automatically built, tested, and deployed.

• Configure automated testing in your CI/CD pipelines to maintain code quality and catch regressions early in the development process.

8. Collaboration Across Geographical Locations

• If your team is geographically distributed, make use of Azure DevOps to bridge the gap. Hold virtual standup meetings, use chat and video conferencing tools, and maintain shared documentation.

9. Documentation and Knowledge Sharing

• Encourage team members to document their work, share knowledge, and contribute to a collective knowledge base.

• Leverage Azure DevOps Wiki to create and maintain documentation related to your projects.

10. Version Control Integration

- Integrate Azure Repos, the version control system within Azure DevOps, with your development tools. This enables seamless version control and code collaboration.

11. Agile Methodologies

- Adopt agile methodologies such as Scrum or Kanban to facilitate iterative development, collaboration, and customer feedback.
- Use Azure Boards to plan and track sprints, backlog items, and release cycles.

Effective team collaboration using Azure DevOps enhances productivity, quality, and transparency in software development projects. By following these best practices, your team can work cohesively, regardless of its size or geographical distribution. In the next section, we will explore the integration of Azure DevOps with Microsoft Teams and other communication tools in more detail.

7.2. Integrating with Microsoft Teams and Other Communication Tools

In today's fast-paced software development environments, effective communication and collaboration are crucial for the success of any project. Azure DevOps recognizes this need and offers integration capabilities with popular communication and collaboration tools, including Microsoft Teams, Slack, and others. In this section, we'll delve into the importance of integrating Azure DevOps with Microsoft Teams and provide insights into leveraging this integration effectively.

1. Why Integrate Azure DevOps with Microsoft Teams?

- **Seamless Collaboration:** Integration with Microsoft Teams allows your development team to collaborate seamlessly by bringing important Azure DevOps notifications and updates directly into your Teams channels. This ensures that everyone is on the same page and can respond promptly to changes and updates.

- **Real-time Notifications:** Receive real-time notifications about work item updates, pull requests, build statuses, and other events directly within your Teams channels. This keeps team members informed without the need to switch between tools.

- **Enhanced Visibility:** With Azure DevOps integration, all team members can access project-related information without leaving the Teams interface. This accessibility boosts visibility into project progress and fosters better decision-making.

- **Reduced Context Switching:** Minimize context switching between Azure DevOps and Teams, allowing developers and other stakeholders to focus on their work without disruptions.

2. Setting Up the Integration

- To set up the integration, start by installing the Azure DevOps app for Microsoft Teams. This app can be found in the Microsoft Teams App Store.

- Once installed, configure the integration by providing the necessary Azure DevOps organization and project details.

- Create dedicated channels in Microsoft Teams for specific projects or teams and configure the Azure DevOps app to post notifications in these channels.

3. Notification Types

- Customize the types of notifications you want to receive in Microsoft Teams. You can choose to receive notifications for various events such as work item updates, code commits, build successes, and more.

- Tailor notifications to your team's needs, ensuring that you receive the right information at the right time.

4. Interactive Bots

- Take advantage of interactive bots that allow you to interact with Azure DevOps directly within Teams. You can use bots to create work items, trigger builds, and perform other actions.

- These bots simplify tasks and streamline the development process by reducing the need to switch between tools.

5. @Mentions and Message Formatting

- Use @mentions to notify specific team members or groups within Teams channels about important Azure DevOps updates or discussions.

• Format messages to include work item details, links to pull requests, and build results. This enhances the clarity of communication within Teams.

6. Managing Access and Permissions

• Ensure that the right team members have access to the integrated Azure DevOps notifications within Teams channels.

• Review and manage permissions to maintain data security and control who can interact with Azure DevOps features within Teams.

7. Best Practices

• Encourage team members to actively participate in discussions within Teams channels. This fosters collaboration and knowledge sharing.

• Set up dedicated Teams channels for different projects or teams to keep discussions and notifications organized.

• Regularly review and update the integration settings to align with changing project requirements.

Integrating Azure DevOps with Microsoft Teams enhances communication and collaboration among development teams. It provides a centralized platform where team members can stay informed about project updates, collaborate on work items, and reduce the friction caused by context switching between tools. By following best practices and leveraging the integration effectively, you can streamline your development processes and improve team productivity. In the following sections, we will explore other aspects of effective collaboration in Azure DevOps, including managing permissions and access control.

7.3. Managing Permissions and Access Control

Effective collaboration within Azure DevOps and integrated communication tools like Microsoft Teams relies on a well-defined permissions and access control strategy. Managing permissions ensures that the right people have the appropriate level of access to resources while maintaining data security and compliance. In this section, we will explore the key aspects of managing permissions and access control within Azure DevOps.

1. Understanding Permissions

- Azure DevOps provides a granular permission model that allows you to control access at various levels, including organizations, projects, repositories, and work items.

- Permissions can be granted to individuals, groups, or teams. You can assign users to predefined roles or create custom roles with specific permissions.

- Common permissions include "Read," "Contribute," "Edit," and "Administer." These permissions determine the level of access users have to different resources.

2. Roles in Azure DevOps

- Azure DevOps offers predefined roles with associated permissions. These roles include "Stakeholder,"

"Contributor," "Reader," "Build Administrators," and more.

• Stakeholders typically have limited access and are suitable for non-developer team members or external stakeholders who need to track progress.

• Contributors have the ability to create and edit work items, participate in discussions, and contribute to code.

• Administrators have full control over a specific resource, such as a project or repository.

• Customize roles to align with your organization's specific needs and structure.

3. Access Control at the Project Level

• At the project level, you can define access control by configuring permissions for teams or individual users.

• Use groups to manage permissions efficiently. For example, you can create a "Developers" group and assign common permissions to all developers.

• Review and update permissions regularly to ensure alignment with project requirements.

4. Branch-Level Permissions

• Azure DevOps allows you to set branch-level permissions to control who can push changes to specific branches within a repository.

• This feature is valuable for maintaining code quality and ensuring that only authorized team members can merge changes into critical branches.

5. Access Control for Repositories

• For repositories, you can specify permissions for individuals or groups, determining who can read, contribute, or administer the repository.

• Consider implementing a "pull request" workflow to ensure that code changes are reviewed and approved before merging.

6. Fine-Grained Work Item Permissions

• Customize permissions for work items to restrict access to specific types of work items or fields.

• This is particularly useful for controlling who can modify certain aspects of a project, such as sensitive customer data.

7. Integration with Identity Providers

• Azure DevOps supports integration with identity providers like Azure Active Directory (AAD). This allows you to manage access through your organization's existing authentication mechanisms.

• Leverage AAD groups to simplify user management and permissions assignment.

8. Audit and Compliance

- Enable audit logging in Azure DevOps to track changes to permissions and access control settings.

- Regularly review audit logs to identify unauthorized access attempts or changes to permissions.

9. Best Practices

- Follow the principle of least privilege (PoLP) to grant users the minimum level of access required to perform their tasks.

- Implement a documented permissions and access control policy to ensure consistency and compliance.

- Educate team members on best practices for managing permissions and the importance of data security.

Effective permissions and access control management in Azure DevOps are essential for maintaining data security, ensuring compliance with regulatory requirements, and facilitating a smooth collaboration process. By understanding the permission model, using predefined roles, and implementing access control at various levels, you can strike a balance between providing access to necessary resources and safeguarding sensitive information. In the next section, we will explore the utilization of dashboards and reporting tools to enhance team communication and decision-making.

7.4. Utilizing Dashboards and Reporting for Team Communication

Dashboards and reporting are indispensable tools in Azure DevOps for enhancing team communication, tracking progress, and making data-driven decisions. In this section, we will delve into the utilization of dashboards and reporting features to optimize your team's workflow and collaboration.

1. Overview of Azure DevOps Dashboards

- Azure DevOps offers customizable dashboards that provide a visual representation of your project's status, progress, and key metrics.

- Dashboards can be tailored to suit specific teams or stakeholders, ensuring that each group has access to the relevant information.

- Widgets are the building blocks of dashboards, and Azure DevOps provides a variety of pre-built widgets for displaying data from different services such as Azure Boards, Azure Repos, Azure Pipelines, and more.

2. Creating Custom Dashboards

- You can create custom dashboards to address the unique needs of your team or project.

- Start by adding widgets to your dashboard. Widgets can display information like burndown charts, build status, code coverage, and work item queries.

• Arrange and configure widgets to provide an at-a-glance view of project health and progress.

3. Sharing Dashboards

• Dashboards can be shared with team members or stakeholders, ensuring that everyone has access to up-to-date information.

• Share dashboards via a URL or make them visible to specific users or groups within your organization.

4. Using Azure DevOps Reporting

• Azure DevOps provides a range of built-in reports that offer insights into various aspects of your project.

• Reports cover areas such as sprint burndown, velocity, release progress, code quality, and more.

• Customize reports to focus on the metrics that matter most to your team.

5. Power BI Integration

• For advanced reporting and data visualization, Azure DevOps integrates with Microsoft Power BI.

• Power BI allows you to create interactive reports and dashboards using data from Azure DevOps.

• This integration provides more flexibility and options for in-depth analysis.

6. Monitoring and Metrics

- Utilize dashboards and reporting to monitor key performance indicators (KPIs) and track project health.

- Regularly review metrics to identify bottlenecks, trends, or areas that require attention.

7. Real-time Collaboration

- Dashboards and reports enable real-time collaboration by providing a shared view of project progress.

- Teams can use this information to make informed decisions and adjust their plans as needed.

8. Best Practices

- Collaborate with your team to define the most relevant dashboards and reports for your project.

- Regularly update dashboards to reflect the current state of the project and avoid displaying outdated information.

- Train team members on how to create, customize, and share dashboards and reports effectively.

- Encourage a culture of transparency and data-driven decision-making within your organization.

By leveraging dashboards and reporting in Azure DevOps, teams can improve communication, increase transparency, and make informed decisions based on real-time data. Whether you are tracking sprint progress, monitoring code quality, or evaluating release readiness, these tools play a vital role in optimizing your DevOps workflow.

In the next section, we will explore best practices for remote and distributed teams, emphasizing effective collaboration and communication in such environments.

7.5. Best Practices for Remote and Distributed Teams

In the modern workplace, remote and distributed teams have become increasingly common, and effective collaboration among team members who may be geographically dispersed is essential. Azure DevOps provides tools and practices to support remote and distributed teams, ensuring that they can work together seamlessly and efficiently. In this section, we will explore best practices for fostering effective collaboration and communication in such environments.

1. Clear Communication Channels

- Establish clear and accessible communication channels for team members to connect and share information. Use tools like Microsoft Teams, Slack, or other chat and video conferencing platforms to facilitate real-time communication.

- Ensure that team members are aware of the preferred communication channels and guidelines for using them. This includes defining when to use chat, video calls, email, or project-related discussions.

2. Regular Standup Meetings

• Conduct regular standup meetings, even in remote setups, to keep everyone aligned and informed about project progress.

• Use video conferencing to enhance the feeling of presence and engagement during standup meetings.

3. Use Azure DevOps for Collaboration

• Leverage Azure DevOps boards, repositories, and pipelines to centralize project-related activities. This allows team members to collaborate within the context of their work.

• Use Azure Boards to track work items, assignments, and progress, providing visibility into who is working on what.

• Collaborate on code in Azure Repos, using pull requests for code review and feedback.

• Automate processes with Azure Pipelines to streamline build and deployment workflows.

4. Documentation and Knowledge Sharing

• Document project-related information, processes, and best practices in a centralized location.

• Encourage team members to share their knowledge and expertise by contributing to documentation and wikis.

• Ensure that documentation is up-to-date and easily accessible to all team members.

5. Time Zone Considerations

• Acknowledge and respect time zone differences within the team. Schedule meetings and deadlines to accommodate the availability of team members in different regions.

• Use scheduling tools that can display multiple time zones to avoid confusion.

6. Effective Use of Agile Practices

• If your team follows Agile methodologies, ensure that Agile ceremonies like sprint planning, retrospectives, and backlog grooming are adapted to remote settings.

• Use Azure Boards to facilitate Agile practices and track sprint progress.

7. Collaborative Tools Integration

• Integrate collaborative tools with Azure DevOps to streamline workflows. For example, you can link Microsoft Teams or Slack channels to Azure DevOps work items, allowing for easy cross-platform communication.

8. Regular Check-Ins

• Conduct regular check-ins with team members to gauge their well-being and address any challenges they may be facing.

- Encourage open and honest communication about remote work experiences.

9. Security and Access Control

- Implement strong security practices to protect sensitive project data.

- Define access control policies in Azure DevOps to ensure that only authorized individuals can access and modify project resources.

10. Continuous Improvement

- Continuously assess and improve remote collaboration practices based on feedback from team members.

- Embrace a culture of continuous improvement to adapt to evolving remote work challenges.

By implementing these best practices, remote and distributed teams can effectively collaborate, maintain productivity, and achieve their project goals in Azure DevOps. Effective communication, documentation, and the use of collaborative tools are key to success in remote work environments, and Azure DevOps provides the necessary features to support these practices. In the next chapter, we will explore the fundamentals of Infrastructure as Code (IaC) with Azure, highlighting its significance in modern DevOps practices.

8.1. Introduction to Infrastructure as Code

In modern software development and DevOps practices, Infrastructure as Code (IaC) has emerged as a crucial concept. IaC enables teams to provision, manage, and configure infrastructure using code and automation, rather than relying on manual processes and configuration. This section provides an introduction to IaC, its significance, and how it fits into the Azure DevOps ecosystem.

What is Infrastructure as Code (IaC)?

Infrastructure as Code (IaC) is an approach that treats infrastructure—such as servers, networks, and databases—as code artifacts. This means that instead of manually configuring servers or using graphical interfaces, infrastructure components are defined, provisioned, and managed through code. IaC allows you to create, modify, and delete infrastructure resources using scripts or code, making the process more predictable, repeatable, and efficient.

Key Concepts in IaC:

1. **Declarative vs. Imperative**: IaC can be declarative, where you specify the desired end state of the infrastructure, or imperative, where you specify the steps to achieve that state. Declarative IaC is often preferred for its simplicity and idempotency.
2. **Idempotency**: Idempotent code ensures that the same action, when performed multiple times, has the same result as doing it once. In IaC, this means that applying the same code repeatedly doesn't cause unintended changes or errors.

3. **Version Control**: IaC code is typically stored in version control systems like Git, enabling tracking changes, collaboration, and rollbacks.
4. **Automation**: IaC emphasizes automation to reduce manual intervention and human errors. Automated provisioning tools like Azure Resource Manager (ARM) templates and Terraform are commonly used.

Why Use Infrastructure as Code?

1. **Consistency**: IaC ensures that infrastructure is created and configured consistently, reducing the risk of configuration drift between environments.
2. **Reproducibility**: With IaC, you can recreate entire infrastructure setups, including servers, networks, and configurations, by running code. This is valuable for disaster recovery and testing.
3. **Scalability**: IaC allows you to scale infrastructure up or down easily by changing code configurations, accommodating changing workload demands.
4. **Collaboration**: IaC code can be version-controlled and shared among team members, promoting collaboration and knowledge sharing.
5. **Auditability**: Changes to infrastructure are documented in code and version history, providing transparency and auditability.

IaC in Azure DevOps

Azure DevOps provides tools and services that seamlessly integrate with IaC practices:

1. **Azure Resource Manager (ARM) Templates**: ARM

templates are JSON files that define Azure resources and their configurations. They can be stored in Azure Repos and used to provision and manage resources in Azure.
2. **Azure DevOps Pipelines**: Azure Pipelines can automate the deployment of IaC templates, allowing you to define CI/CD pipelines for infrastructure changes.
3. **Terraform**: While not an Azure-specific tool, Terraform is a popular choice for multi-cloud and hybrid cloud environments. You can use Terraform with Azure DevOps for IaC provisioning.
4. **Testing and Validation**: Azure DevOps can be used to run tests and validation checks on IaC code to catch errors before provisioning resources.
5. **Governance and Compliance**: Azure DevOps integrates with Azure Policy and Azure Blueprints to enforce governance and compliance rules on IaC deployments.

In the following sections, we will delve deeper into using IaC with Azure DevOps, exploring best practices, common tools, and integration scenarios.

8.2. Azure Resource Manager (ARM) Templates

Azure Resource Manager (ARM) templates are a fundamental component of Infrastructure as Code (IaC) in the Azure ecosystem. These templates are JSON files that define the infrastructure and resources needed for your application or solution. In this section, we will explore ARM templates in depth, including their structure, key concepts, and how to use them effectively within Azure DevOps.

Structure of ARM Templates

An ARM template consists of the following sections:

1. **Schema**: Specifies the version of the ARM template schema being used.
2. **Content Version**: A user-defined version number for the template.
3. **Parameters**: Defines input parameters that allow customization of the template.
4. **Variables**: Contains user-defined variables used within the template.
5. **Functions**: ARM templates support various built-in functions for data manipulation and transformation.
6. **Resources**: The most critical section, where you define the Azure resources to be created or configured. Each resource is defined using a resource type, name, and properties.
7. **Outputs**: Provides the ability to retrieve and display information about the resources created by the template.

Key Concepts in ARM Templates

Resource Types

Resource types are defined using a namespace, type, and API version. For example, "type": "Microsoft.Compute/virtualMachines" defines a virtual machine resource.

Parameters

Parameters allow you to customize the template when deploying it. They act as input values that can vary from one deployment to another. For example, you can define a parameter for the VM size or the number of instances.

Variables

Variables enable you to store and reuse values or expressions within the template. This can simplify complex configurations and make templates more maintainable.

Functions

ARM templates provide various functions for working with data, including arithmetic, string manipulation, and conditional logic. Functions can be used to calculate values or construct resource names dynamically.

Outputs

Outputs define values that you want to retrieve and display after the template is deployed. These can be useful for obtaining resource identifiers or connection strings for further configuration.

Benefits of ARM Templates

1. **Infrastructure as Code**: ARM templates allow you to define and manage your infrastructure using code, ensuring consistency and reproducibility.
2. **Version Control**: Templates can be stored in version control systems like Azure Repos, enabling collaboration and tracking changes over time.
3. **Automation**: Azure DevOps Pipelines can automate the deployment of ARM templates, providing a reliable and

repeatable process.

4. **Modularity**: Templates can be broken down into smaller, reusable components, making it easier to manage complex infrastructure setups.
5. **Scalability**: ARM templates can be parameterized to handle varying workloads and scaling requirements.

Using ARM Templates in Azure DevOps

Azure DevOps provides native support for ARM templates, allowing you to seamlessly integrate infrastructure deployments into your CI/CD pipelines. Here's an overview of the process:

1. **Author ARM Templates**: Create ARM templates that define your infrastructure and resources.
2. **Store in Version Control**: Store your ARM templates in Azure Repos or any other version control system of your choice.
3. **Define Parameters**: Define parameters for your templates to allow customization during deployment.
4. **Create Deployment Pipeline**: Set up an Azure DevOps Pipeline that includes a deployment job for your ARM templates.
5. **Parameterize Deployments**: Configure the pipeline to accept parameter values for each deployment stage.
6. **Automate Deployments**: Use tasks and scripts within the pipeline to deploy ARM templates to Azure.
7. **Testing and Validation**: Include validation steps to ensure that the deployed infrastructure meets your requirements.
8. **Monitoring and Reporting**: Implement monitoring and reporting solutions to track the performance and health of your infrastructure.

In the subsequent sections, we will dive deeper into practical aspects of working with ARM templates, including best practices, advanced scenarios, and troubleshooting tips.

8.3. Integrating IaC into Azure DevOps Pipelines

Integrating Infrastructure as Code (IaC) into Azure DevOps Pipelines is a crucial step in automating and managing your Azure infrastructure deployments efficiently. In this section, we will explore how to seamlessly incorporate IaC practices into your CI/CD workflows using Azure DevOps.

Leveraging Azure DevOps for IaC

Azure DevOps provides a comprehensive set of tools and services that facilitate the adoption of IaC principles. Here's a step-by-step guide on how to integrate IaC into your Azure DevOps Pipelines:

1. Create an Azure DevOps Repository

If you haven't already, set up an Azure DevOps repository to store your Infrastructure as Code (IaC) templates. You can choose between Azure Repos, GitHub, or other supported version control systems.

2. Author ARM Templates

Write Azure Resource Manager (ARM) templates that define your infrastructure in code. These templates should be stored in the repository created in the previous step. Make sure to follow best practices for ARM template design.

3. Define Parameterization

Use parameterization in your ARM templates to allow for customization during deployment. Parameters can be used to specify things like resource names, sizes, and configurations.

4. Set Up Azure DevOps Pipelines

Create an Azure DevOps Pipeline for your IaC project. You can define pipelines using YAML or through the visual interface, depending on your preference and project requirements.

5. YAML Pipeline Example

Here's an example of a YAML-based Azure DevOps Pipeline for deploying ARM templates:

```
trigger:

- '*'

pool:

vmImage: 'windows-latest'

variables:

- group: MyAzureServiceConnection

steps:

- task: UsePythonVersion@0

inputs:

versionSpec: '3.x'
```

addToPath: true

- script: |

az login—service-principal -u $(servicePrincipalId) -p $(servicePrincipalKey)—tenant $(tenantId)

az account set—subscription $(subscriptionId)

displayName: 'Azure Login'

- task: AzureResourceManagerTemplateDeployment@3

inputs:

deploymentScope: 'Resource Group'

action: 'Create Or Update Resource Group'

resourceGroupName: $(resourceGroupName)

location: 'East US'

templateLocation: 'Linked artifact'

csmFile: 'path/to/your/arm-template.json'

csmParametersFile: 'path/to/your/parameters.json'

deploymentMode: 'Incremental'

This YAML pipeline example includes the following key steps:

- It triggers on any changes in the repository.
- It uses a predefined Azure service connection for authentication.
- It logs in to Azure using service principal credentials.

- It deploys an ARM template to create or update a resource group in the specified Azure location.

6. Parameterize Deployments

In your pipeline, make sure to parameterize deployments so that you can specify different parameter values for different environments (e.g., development, staging, production).

7. Automate Testing and Validation

Include testing and validation steps in your pipeline to ensure that the deployed infrastructure meets your requirements. This can include running automated tests on your resources, checking for compliance with security policies, and validating configurations.

8. Implement Rollback Strategies

Plan for rollback strategies in case deployments encounter issues. Azure DevOps allows you to define and trigger rollback actions automatically when errors occur during deployment.

9. Monitor and Alert

Implement monitoring and alerting solutions to track the performance and health of your deployed infrastructure. Azure Monitor and Application Insights are valuable tools for this purpose.

10. Continuous Improvement

Regularly review and refine your IaC practices in Azure DevOps pipelines to adapt to changing requirements and best practices in the DevOps and cloud infrastructure space.

By following these steps, you can effectively integrate Infrastructure as Code into your Azure DevOps Pipelines, promoting automation, consistency, and reliability in your Azure deployments.

8.4. Managing Infrastructure Deployment and Configuration

Once you have integrated Infrastructure as Code (IaC) into your Azure DevOps Pipelines, the next crucial aspect is managing the deployment and configuration of your infrastructure. This section delves into the key strategies and best practices for effectively managing these aspects within your DevOps processes.

Deployment Strategies

1. Incremental Deployments

One common approach is to use incremental deployments when managing infrastructure. With incremental deployments, only the necessary changes are applied during updates. This reduces the risk of disrupting your services and makes it easier to track changes over time. Azure DevOps Pipelines allow you to specify the deployment mode as "Incremental" in your ARM template deployment tasks.

2. Blue-Green Deployments

For more complex setups, consider implementing blue-green deployments. This strategy involves running two identical environments (blue and green) simultaneously. When updates are needed, you switch traffic to the updated environment (green), allowing you to validate changes and easily roll back if issues arise. Azure Traffic Manager can help manage this process.

Configuration Management

3. Configuration Drift Prevention

Configuration drift can occur when changes are made to infrastructure resources outside of your IaC process. To prevent drift, enforce policies and use Azure Policy or Azure Governance to automatically remediate any configuration changes that violate your policies.

4. Infrastructure as Code (IaC) Updates

As your infrastructure evolves, you'll need to update your IaC templates to reflect changes in requirements or configurations. Use version control for your IaC templates and track changes diligently. Ensure that your pipelines automatically trigger updates when changes are pushed to the repository.

Monitoring and Logging

5. *Azure Monitor*

Implement Azure Monitor to gain insights into your infrastructure's performance, availability, and health. Configure alerts to proactively respond to issues and set up log analytics to centralize log data for analysis.

6. *Application Insights*

For applications running on your infrastructure, leverage Application Insights to monitor and troubleshoot application performance. Integrating Application Insights with your application code provides valuable telemetry data.

Disaster Recovery and High Availability

7. *Disaster Recovery Planning*

Plan for disaster recovery by creating a robust backup and recovery strategy. Azure offers various solutions like Azure Site Recovery and Azure Backup to ensure data and service availability in the event of a disaster.

8. *High Availability (HA) Architectures*

Design your infrastructure with high availability in mind. Distribute resources across multiple Azure regions and use load balancers to ensure service continuity. Implementing Availability Zones and redundant configurations can enhance HA.

Scaling and Optimization

9. Auto-Scaling

Implement auto-scaling based on metrics such as CPU usage, memory, or custom metrics. Azure provides tools like Azure Autoscale and Virtual Machine Scale Sets to automatically adjust resource capacity to match demand.

10. Cost Optimization

Regularly review and optimize your infrastructure to minimize costs. Azure Cost Management and Billing help track expenses, while rightsizing resources and using reserved instances can lead to cost savings.

Infrastructure as Code (IaC) Governance

11. Policy Enforcement

Leverage Azure Policy to enforce governance and compliance rules across your Azure environment. Define policies that align with your organization's requirements and automatically enforce them.

12. Role-Based Access Control (RBAC)

Implement RBAC to manage permissions and access control for Azure resources. Assign roles based on job responsibilities and follow the principle of least privilege to enhance security.

Documentation and Collaboration

13. Documentation

Maintain thorough documentation of your infrastructure, including architecture diagrams, IaC templates, and operational procedures. Documentation is crucial for onboarding new team members and troubleshooting.

14. Collaboration

Promote collaboration among development, operations, and security teams. Azure DevOps supports integration with collaboration tools like Microsoft Teams, Slack, and more, facilitating communication and coordination.

By implementing these strategies and best practices, you can effectively manage infrastructure deployment and configuration within your Azure DevOps processes, ensuring reliability, security, and scalability for your applications and services.

8.5. Security and Compliance in IaC

Security and compliance are paramount when managing infrastructure through Infrastructure as Code (IaC) in Azure DevOps. This section explores the key considerations, best practices, and tools to ensure your IaC deployments are secure and compliant with industry standards and organizational policies.

Security Best Practices

1. Secure Credentials and Secrets

Avoid hardcoding credentials or secrets in your IaC templates. Leverage Azure Key Vault to securely store and retrieve sensitive information. Refer to these secrets dynamically in your templates to minimize exposure.

2. Role-Based Access Control (RBAC)

Implement RBAC to control access to Azure resources. Assign roles with the principle of least privilege, ensuring that users and service principals have only the permissions they need.

3. Network Security

Define strict network security rules to control incoming and outgoing traffic to your resources. Azure Network Security Groups (NSGs) and Azure Firewall can help you manage network access effectively.

4. Continuous Scanning

Integrate vulnerability scanning tools into your pipelines to continuously scan your infrastructure code for security vulnerabilities. Tools like Azure Security Center and third-party solutions can identify and remediate potential issues.

Compliance and Governance

5. Compliance Policies

Establish compliance policies that align with industry standards and regulatory requirements. Azure Policy and Azure Blueprints enable you to define and enforce policies across your infrastructure.

6. Auditing and Logging

Enable auditing and logging for your Azure resources. Azure Monitor and Azure Security Center provide insights into security events and allow you to investigate incidents effectively.

7. Security Baselines

Define security baselines for your infrastructure, including configurations, patch levels, and security policies. Use tools like Azure Security Benchmark and Azure Policy initiatives to ensure compliance with these baselines.

Infrastructure Testing

8. Security Testing

Incorporate security testing into your pipeline to identify vulnerabilities and weaknesses in your infrastructure. Tools like Azure DevOps Security Scanner can assist in identifying security issues.

9. Compliance Testing

Perform compliance testing to verify that your infrastructure adheres to established policies and standards. Automate these tests to ensure ongoing compliance.

Documentation and Training

10. Documentation

Maintain detailed documentation of your security and compliance practices. Document security controls, policies, and incident response procedures to facilitate audits and investigations.

11. Training

Provide training to your team members to keep them updated on security best practices. Training ensures that everyone understands their roles and responsibilities in maintaining a secure infrastructure.

Incident Response

12. Incident Response Plan

Develop an incident response plan that outlines steps to be taken in case of a security breach. Test the plan regularly to ensure a swift and effective response.

13. Security Culture

Promote a security-conscious culture within your organization. Encourage employees to report security concerns promptly and reward good security practices.

By following these security and compliance best practices, you can enhance the security of your Infrastructure as Code deployments in Azure DevOps. Building security into your IaC processes helps safeguard your infrastructure, data, and applications against evolving threats and ensures alignment with regulatory requirements.

Chapter 9: Monitoring and Performance Optimization

9.1. Introduction to Monitoring in Azure DevOps

Monitoring is an essential aspect of modern software development and operations. It allows organizations to track the performance, availability, and health of their applications and infrastructure. In the context of Azure DevOps, monitoring plays a crucial role in ensuring the reliability of applications and services deployed on Azure.

The Importance of Monitoring

Effective monitoring provides several benefits, including:

1. **Proactive Issue Detection**: Monitoring allows you to identify issues before they impact users. By setting up alerts and thresholds, you can receive notifications when key metrics deviate from expected values.
2. **Performance Optimization**: Monitoring helps you understand how your applications and services are performing. It provides insights into resource utilization, response times, and bottlenecks, allowing you to optimize performance.
3. **Troubleshooting and Debugging**: When issues do occur, monitoring data can be invaluable for troubleshooting. It provides a historical record of events and performance metrics, making it easier to diagnose problems.
4. **Capacity Planning**: By analyzing monitoring data, you can make informed decisions about scaling your infrastructure. This ensures that your applications can

handle increased load and traffic.

Monitoring in Azure DevOps

Azure DevOps offers a range of tools and services for monitoring applications and infrastructure. These include:

- **Azure Monitor**: Azure Monitor is a comprehensive monitoring solution that provides insights into the performance and health of your Azure resources. It collects telemetry data from various sources, including applications, virtual machines, and Azure services.

- **Application Insights**: Application Insights is a service that helps you monitor the performance and usage of your applications. It provides real-time telemetry data, including request rates, response times, and error rates.

- **Log Analytics**: Log Analytics allows you to collect and analyze log data from various sources, such as virtual machines, containers, and Azure services. It provides powerful querying and visualization capabilities.

- **Azure Metrics**: Azure Metrics provides a unified view of performance metrics for Azure resources. You can set up alerts based on these metrics to receive notifications when thresholds are breached.

- **Azure Application Service Diagnostics**: This service is tailored for web applications hosted on Azure App Service. It provides diagnostics and troubleshooting capabilities, including detailed error messages and performance data.

Key Monitoring Scenarios

When implementing monitoring in Azure DevOps, consider the following key scenarios:

1. **Application Performance Monitoring**: Monitor the performance of your applications to ensure they meet performance objectives. Track response times, error rates, and resource utilization.
2. **Infrastructure Monitoring**: Monitor the health and availability of your infrastructure, including virtual machines, databases, and networking components.
3. **Log and Event Monitoring**: Collect and analyze logs and events generated by your applications and infrastructure. This can help you identify issues and security incidents.
4. **Alerting and Notification**: Set up alerts and notifications to proactively detect and respond to issues. Define alerting thresholds and escalation policies.
5. **Capacity Planning**: Use monitoring data to plan for resource scaling and capacity adjustments based on usage patterns and trends.
6. **Security Monitoring**: Implement security monitoring to detect and respond to security threats and vulnerabilities. Monitor for unusual activities and unauthorized access.

In the subsequent sections of this chapter, we will dive deeper into various aspects of monitoring in Azure DevOps, including specific tools and best practices for performance optimization and proactive issue detection. Monitoring is a critical component of DevOps practices, enabling teams to deliver high-quality software with confidence.

9.2. Implementing Application Insights

Application Insights is a powerful service provided by Azure for monitoring and gaining insights into the performance and usage of your applications. It's particularly well-suited for web applications, APIs, and microservices hosted on Azure, but it can also be used for applications running on other platforms. In this section, we'll explore how to implement Application Insights to enhance your monitoring capabilities in Azure DevOps.

Setting Up Application Insights

To get started with Application Insights:

1. **Create an Application Insights Resource**: In the Azure portal, create a new Application Insights resource. You can specify the region and other configuration settings based on your application's requirements.
2. **Instrument Your Application**: To monitor an application, you need to instrument it with the Application Insights SDK. The SDK is available for various programming languages, including .NET, Java, JavaScript, and more. Instrumentation involves adding code to your application to collect telemetry data.
3. **Configure Telemetry Collection**: Application Insights automatically collects telemetry data, including request traces, exceptions, dependency calls, and custom events. You can configure which types of data to collect and how long to retain it.
4. **Integrate with Azure Services**: Application Insights seamlessly integrates with other Azure services, such as Azure Monitor and Azure DevOps. This integration allows you to correlate application performance with

infrastructure health and perform advanced analytics.

Key Features of Application Insights

Application Insights offers a range of features to help you monitor and troubleshoot your applications:

- **Performance Monitoring**: Application Insights tracks the response times of requests and helps identify slow or failing operations. It provides insights into server-side and client-side performance.

- **Error Tracking**: The service automatically detects and logs exceptions and errors, making it easier to identify and fix issues in your application's code.

- **Dependency Tracking**: Application Insights can trace dependencies between different components of your application, such as API calls, database queries, and external services.

- **Request Tracking**: You can see detailed information about incoming requests, including user sessions, user agents, and geographic locations.

- **Custom Telemetry**: Besides automatic telemetry, you can also send custom telemetry data, allowing you to track specific events, usage patterns, or business metrics.

- **Analytics and Querying**: Application Insights includes a powerful query language that allows you to analyze telemetry data, create custom dashboards, and set up alerts based on specific conditions.

Monitoring Dashboards

Once you have instrumented your application and configured Application Insights, you can access monitoring dashboards that provide real-time insights into your application's performance and usage. These dashboards display information such as:

- **Response times**: Monitor the time it takes for your application to respond to requests.
- **Failure rates**: Track the percentage of failed requests or exceptions occurring in your application.
- **Dependency calls**: Visualize the dependencies between different components of your application and identify bottlenecks.
- **User sessions**: Understand how users are interacting with your application, including their geographic locations and usage patterns.
- **Custom metrics**: Create custom charts and metrics based on the telemetry data you collect.

Integration with Azure DevOps

Application Insights integrates seamlessly with Azure DevOps, allowing you to:

- **Create Work Items**: When Application Insights detects issues, such as exceptions or slow response times, you can create work items directly in Azure DevOps for your development team to address.

- **Link to Code**: Work items can be linked to specific code changes, making it easy to track the resolution of issues.

- **Continuous Monitoring**: Set up alerts in Application Insights to notify your team in Azure DevOps when certain conditions are met, such as a high error rate or slow response times.

- **Release Annotations**: Application Insights can create release annotations in Azure DevOps, providing a timeline of application deployments and allowing you to correlate changes with performance issues.

Best Practices

To make the most of Application Insights, consider the following best practices:

- **Instrument Early**: Start instrumenting your application with Application Insights from the beginning of your development process to capture valuable data from day one.

- **Use Custom Telemetry**: Leverage custom telemetry to track application-specific events and metrics that are important to your business.

- **Set Up Alerts**: Configure alerts based on meaningful thresholds to proactively detect and address issues.

- **Monitor User Sessions**: Understand how users interact with your application to improve user experience.

- **Leverage Analytics**: Use the querying and analytics capabilities of Application Insights to gain deeper insights and create custom dashboards.

Application Insights is a valuable tool for monitoring and improving the performance and reliability of your applications. When integrated with Azure DevOps, it provides a holistic approach to managing and maintaining your software projects. In the following sections, we'll explore other monitoring and optimization strategies within Azure DevOps.

9.3. Azure Monitor and Log Analytics

Azure Monitor is a comprehensive monitoring and analytics service provided by Microsoft Azure. It enables you to collect and analyze telemetry data from various Azure resources, applications, and infrastructure components. In this section, we will delve into Azure Monitor and its integration with Log Analytics, a powerful tool for querying and analyzing data collected by Azure Monitor.

Azure Monitor Components

Azure Monitor comprises several key components:

1. **Metrics**: Azure Monitor collects metrics data from various Azure resources, such as virtual machines, databases, and web apps. These metrics provide insights into the health and performance of your resources. You can configure alerts based on metric data to receive notifications when predefined thresholds are breached.
2. **Logs**: Azure Monitor also collects log data, including diagnostic logs, activity logs, and custom logs. Diagnostic logs capture detailed information about resource

operations, while activity logs record actions performed on resources. Custom logs allow you to send application-specific log data for analysis.

3. **Alerts**: You can create alerts in Azure Monitor to notify you of important events or conditions, such as a virtual machine reaching high CPU utilization or a failed deployment.
4. **Workbooks**: Workbooks are customizable dashboards that allow you to visualize and analyze metrics and log data from multiple sources in one place. You can create custom workbooks tailored to your monitoring needs.
5. **Application Insights**: As mentioned in the previous section, Application Insights is a part of Azure Monitor, focusing on application-level monitoring, including performance, errors, and user interactions.

Log Analytics

Log Analytics is a powerful query and analysis tool that works seamlessly with Azure Monitor. It allows you to query large volumes of log data from various sources using a query language called Kusto Query Language (KQL).

Key features of Log Analytics include:

- **Custom Log Data**: You can ingest custom log data into Log Analytics from sources like applications, virtual machines, and containers. This data can be queried alongside other telemetry data.

- **Query Language**: Kusto Query Language (KQL) is a versatile query language that enables you to filter, aggregate, and analyze log data. You can create complex queries to extract meaningful insights.

• **Dashboards**: Log Analytics provides customizable dashboards where you can pin query results, charts, and other visualizations for real-time monitoring.

• **Alerting**: You can set up alerts in Log Analytics to trigger notifications or automated actions when specific conditions are met in your log data. This can be particularly useful for identifying security threats or operational issues.

Using Log Analytics with Azure Monitor

To use Log Analytics effectively with Azure Monitor, follow these steps:

1. **Configure Data Sources**: Decide which data sources you want to collect and analyze in Azure Monitor. Configure diagnostic settings on Azure resources to send telemetry data to Azure Monitor.
2. **Create Log Analytics Workspace**: Create a Log Analytics workspace in the Azure portal. This workspace will serve as the central repository for log data.
3. **Write Queries**: Use KQL queries to filter, transform, and analyze log data in the Log Analytics workspace. Queries can help you identify trends, troubleshoot issues, and gain insights into resource performance.
4. **Create Alerts**: Set up alerts based on query results to receive notifications when specific conditions are met. This proactive approach allows you to address issues promptly.
5. **Custom Dashboards**: Create custom dashboards in Log Analytics or use Azure Dashboards to visualize key metrics and query results.

Example KQL Query

Here's a simple example of a KQL query that retrieves the count of error logs from an Azure virtual machine's diagnostic logs over the last hour:

```
Heartbeat

| where TimeGenerated >= ago(1h)

| where Resource == "<VM Resource ID>"

| where Category == "Errors"

| count
```

In this query:

- Heartbeat is the data source.
- TimeGenerated is used to filter data from the last hour.
- Resource is filtered to the specific virtual machine.
- Category is filtered to errors.
- count counts the matching log entries.

Azure Monitor and Log Analytics provide a robust solution for monitoring, analyzing, and responding to telemetry data from Azure resources and applications. This integration plays a crucial role in ensuring the reliability and performance of your Azure-based systems. In the next section, we'll explore performance tuning and optimization strategies.

9.4. Performance Tuning and Optimization Strategies

Performance tuning and optimization are essential aspects of managing and maintaining Azure-based applications and services. In this section, we will explore various strategies and best practices for ensuring that your Azure resources perform efficiently and deliver a great user experience.

1. Right-Sizing Resources

One of the fundamental steps in optimizing performance is right-sizing your Azure resources. This involves selecting the appropriate size (SKU) for virtual machines, databases, and other resources. Azure provides a variety of options, and choosing the right size based on your workload requirements can significantly impact performance and cost. Regularly review and adjust resource sizes as needed to meet changing demands.

2. Monitoring and Benchmarking

Continuous monitoring and benchmarking are crucial for identifying performance bottlenecks and anomalies. Azure Monitor, as discussed earlier, enables you to collect telemetry data and set up alerts. Use this data to proactively identify issues and trends. Benchmarking involves comparing your application's performance against predefined performance metrics to ensure it meets expected standards.

3. Database Optimization

If your application relies on databases, optimize database performance by indexing tables, using appropriate query patterns, and ensuring efficient data storage. Azure offers services like Azure

SQL Database and Azure Cosmos DB, which provide performance optimization features, such as auto-tuning and scaling.

4. Content Delivery Networks (CDNs)

Leverage Azure Content Delivery Network (CDN) to cache and deliver content to users from edge locations worldwide. CDNs reduce latency and improve the responsiveness of web applications by serving static assets, such as images and scripts, from the nearest edge location.

5. Load Balancing

Distribute incoming traffic across multiple instances of your application using Azure Load Balancer or Azure Application Gateway. Load balancing enhances availability and ensures that no single instance is overwhelmed, leading to improved performance and fault tolerance.

6. Caching

Implement caching mechanisms to store frequently accessed data in-memory. Azure Cache for Redis is a managed caching service that can significantly reduce the load on your databases and improve response times for read-heavy workloads.

7. Optimizing Storage

Azure offers various storage options, including Azure Blob Storage, Azure Files, and Azure Disk Storage. Optimize storage performance by selecting the appropriate storage type and tier based on your data access patterns and performance requirements.

8. Content Compression

Enable content compression for web applications to reduce the amount of data transmitted over the network. Azure Application Gateway and Azure Front Door provide built-in support for content compression.

9. Auto-Scaling

Implement auto-scaling policies to automatically adjust the number of resources based on demand. Azure Auto Scaling enables your application to handle traffic spikes and scale down during periods of low usage, optimizing cost and performance.

10. Database Sharding

For applications with rapidly growing databases, consider database sharding. Sharding involves distributing data across multiple database instances to improve query performance and scalability. Azure offers tools like Azure SQL Database Hyperscale for automatic sharding.

11. Network Performance

Optimize network performance by choosing the right Azure Virtual Network topology, implementing Azure ExpressRoute for dedicated network connectivity, and configuring network security groups (NSGs) to allow traffic efficiently.

12. Azure Functions and Serverless

Consider using Azure Functions and serverless computing for workloads that have sporadic or unpredictable usage patterns. Azure Functions automatically scale based on demand and can be cost-effective for certain scenarios.

13. Application-Level Optimization

Review and optimize your application code for performance. Identify and eliminate inefficient code, reduce database queries, and leverage asynchronous processing where appropriate.

14. Proactive Monitoring

Set up proactive monitoring and alerting to detect performance degradation or anomalies before they impact users. Azure Application Insights and Log Analytics play a crucial role in this regard.

15. Regular Testing and Tuning

Perform regular load testing and profiling to identify performance bottlenecks and areas for improvement. Use tools like Azure DevTest Labs to simulate real-world usage scenarios.

Performance tuning and optimization in Azure are ongoing processes that require continuous monitoring and adjustments. By following these best practices and leveraging Azure's performance-related services, you can ensure that your applications and services deliver the best possible experience to users while optimizing costs. In the next section, we will explore proactive monitoring and alerting in more detail.

9.5. Proactive Monitoring and Alerting

Proactive monitoring and alerting are critical components of a robust Azure DevOps strategy. They allow you to detect issues and potential problems before they impact your applications or services, enabling you to take timely action and maintain high availability and performance. In this section, we will delve into the importance of proactive monitoring and how to set up effective alerting mechanisms within your Azure environment.

1. Understanding Proactive Monitoring

Proactive monitoring involves continuously monitoring various aspects of your Azure resources, including virtual machines, databases, web applications, and more. It aims to identify abnormal patterns, performance degradation, and potential bottlenecks in real-time or near-real-time. By staying ahead of issues, you can minimize downtime, reduce user impact, and maintain a positive user experience.

2. Azure Monitor

Azure Monitor is a comprehensive monitoring solution provided by Microsoft Azure. It enables you to collect telemetry data from various Azure resources and applications. Azure Monitor offers the following essential components:

- **Metrics**: Azure Monitor Metrics provide numerical data about the performance and health of your resources. You can set up alerts based on specific metric thresholds. For example, you can create an alert for CPU utilization exceeding 90% for a sustained period.

- **Logs**: Azure Monitor Logs (formerly known as Azure Log Analytics) allow you to collect, analyze, and act on log data from your applications and resources. You can create custom queries and set up alerts based on log data, helping you identify issues or security threats.

- **Application Insights**: Azure Application Insights is designed for monitoring web applications. It provides in-depth insights into your application's performance, dependencies, and user behavior. You can set up alerts for application-specific issues, such as slow response times or failed requests.

• **Activity Logs**: Azure Activity Logs capture all the activities and events within your Azure subscription. You can use Activity Log alerts to monitor changes made to your resources, helping you maintain security and compliance.

3. Setting Up Alerts

Effective alerting is a crucial part of proactive monitoring. Azure Monitor allows you to create alerts based on metrics, logs, or activity log events. When setting up alerts, consider the following best practices:

• **Define Clear Alert Criteria**: Clearly define the conditions that trigger an alert. For example, specify the threshold for CPU usage or the frequency of specific log events.

• **Use Dynamic Thresholds**: In some cases, it's beneficial to use dynamic thresholds that adjust based on historical data or seasonal variations in your workload.

• **Multiple Alert Channels**: Configure alerts to notify multiple channels, such as email, SMS, or integration with incident management tools like Microsoft Teams or Slack. This ensures that the right people are notified promptly.

• **Alerting Hierarchy**: Establish an alerting hierarchy, indicating who should be alerted first and who should be notified as a backup. This hierarchy ensures that alerts are addressed promptly.

• **Escalation Policies**: Implement escalation policies to handle situations where the initial alert is not acknowledged or resolved within a specified timeframe.

• **Testing Alerts**: Regularly test your alerting mechanisms to ensure they function correctly. Simulate scenarios to verify that alerts are triggered when expected.

• **Documentation**: Maintain documentation that includes alerting procedures, contact information, and response plans. This documentation is invaluable during incident response.

4. Actionable Alerts

Not all alerts are created equal. Some alerts may require immediate action, while others can be informative. Ensure that your alerts are actionable and provide sufficient information to diagnose and resolve issues quickly. Include relevant details in alert notifications, such as the affected resource, the nature of the problem, and potential mitigation steps.

5. Continuous Improvement

Proactive monitoring and alerting are not static processes. They require continuous refinement and improvement. Regularly review your alerting configurations to ensure they remain aligned with your application's evolving requirements. Adjust alert thresholds and conditions based on changing performance expectations.

By implementing proactive monitoring and effective alerting in your Azure DevOps practices, you can enhance the reliability and performance of your applications while minimizing the impact of unexpected issues. These practices play a crucial role in maintaining a seamless user experience and upholding service-level agreements (SLAs). In the next chapter, we will explore security considerations within Azure DevOps.

10.1. Understanding Security within Azure DevOps

Security is a paramount concern in modern software development and operations. Azure DevOps provides a robust set of features and best practices to help you build and maintain secure DevOps pipelines. In this section, we will delve into the fundamental aspects of security within Azure DevOps, including the importance of security, secure development practices, secrets management, compliance, and security scanning.

Importance of Security

Security breaches can have severe consequences, including data leaks, financial losses, damage to reputation, and legal implications. As organizations embrace DevOps practices, they must prioritize security throughout the software development lifecycle (SDLC). Azure DevOps empowers teams to adopt a security-first mindset by integrating security measures into their workflows.

Secure Development Practices

Secure development practices involve incorporating security checks and measures into every phase of the SDLC. Azure DevOps offers several features to support secure development:

- **Static Application Security Testing (SAST)**: SAST tools analyze source code for security vulnerabilities. Azure DevOps integrates with various SAST tools, allowing you to scan your code for issues like SQL injection, cross-site scripting (XSS), and more.

- **Dynamic Application Security Testing (DAST)**: DAST tools test your running application for vulnerabilities by sending simulated attacks. You can automate DAST testing as part of your release pipeline.

- **Dependency Scanning**: Azure DevOps can scan your dependencies for known vulnerabilities. By keeping dependencies up to date and addressing security issues promptly, you reduce the risk of vulnerabilities in your applications.

Secrets Management

Managing sensitive information, such as API keys, connection strings, and certificates, is crucial for security. Azure DevOps provides tools to manage secrets securely:

- **Azure Key Vault Integration**: Azure Key Vault is a cloud-based service for managing cryptographic keys and secrets. You can integrate Azure Key Vault with Azure DevOps to store and retrieve secrets securely during CI/CD processes.

- **Variable Groups**: Variable groups in Azure DevOps allow you to store and manage secrets centrally. You can link variable groups to pipelines and restrict access to authorized personnel.

Compliance and Governance

Compliance with industry regulations and organizational policies is vital. Azure DevOps helps maintain compliance through the following features:

- **Policies**: Azure DevOps allows you to define policies that enforce code quality, security checks, and compliance standards. Policies can prevent deployments that don't meet your criteria.

- **Audit Logs**: Azure DevOps generates audit logs that record activities in your organization. You can use these logs for compliance and troubleshooting.

Security Scanning and Threat Mitigation

Continuous security scanning and threat mitigation are essential for identifying and addressing security risks:

- **Container Scanning**: If you use containers, you can integrate container scanning into your CI/CD pipelines. This helps identify vulnerabilities in container images.

- **Security Work Items**: Azure DevOps can create work items for security issues detected during scans. This ensures that security vulnerabilities are tracked and addressed.

- **Threat Modeling**: Incorporate threat modeling into your development process to proactively identify and mitigate security risks.

By embracing security practices within Azure DevOps, you can enhance the security posture of your applications and infrastructure. Security should be an integral part of your DevOps culture, and Azure DevOps provides the tools and capabilities to achieve that goal. In the next section, we will explore Azure Key Vault and secrets management in more detail.

10.2. Implementing Secure Development Practices in Azure DevOps

Implementing secure development practices in Azure DevOps is crucial to identify and mitigate security vulnerabilities throughout the software development lifecycle. In this section, we'll delve into specific measures and tools available in Azure DevOps to ensure the security of your code and applications.

Static Application Security Testing (SAST)

Static Application Security Testing, or SAST, is a critical practice for identifying vulnerabilities in your source code before it's even executed. Azure DevOps provides integration with various SAST tools, such as Veracode, Checkmarx, and Fortify, allowing you to perform automated code scans during your CI/CD pipelines.

By incorporating SAST into your CI/CD processes, you can automatically analyze your codebase for security issues like SQL injection, cross-site scripting (XSS), and insecure coding practices. When vulnerabilities are detected, you can set up policies to prevent vulnerable code from being deployed, ensuring that security checks are an integral part of your release pipeline.

Dynamic Application Security Testing (DAST)

While SAST checks your code statically, Dynamic Application Security Testing (DAST) focuses on identifying vulnerabilities in your running application. Azure DevOps enables you to automate DAST scans as part of your release pipeline to assess your application's security posture in real-world conditions.

Tools like OWASP ZAP and Qualys Web Application Scanning can be integrated into Azure DevOps to perform DAST scans. These scans simulate attacks on your application to discover issues like injection attacks, broken authentication, and security misconfigurations. Integrating DAST into your CI/CD process ensures that security testing is conducted on the deployed application.

Dependency Scanning

Managing dependencies is a critical aspect of secure development. Outdated or vulnerable dependencies can introduce security risks into your applications. Azure DevOps provides dependency scanning capabilities that check your project's dependencies against known vulnerabilities.

By keeping your dependencies up to date and addressing vulnerabilities promptly, you reduce the attack surface of your application. Azure DevOps can automatically create work items for vulnerable dependencies, allowing your team to prioritize and remediate issues efficiently.

Secure Coding Standards

Enforcing secure coding standards is essential for reducing the likelihood of introducing vulnerabilities in your codebase. Azure DevOps allows you to define coding standards and best practices using policies and static code analysis tools.

For example, you can set up policies that require code to adhere to specific security guidelines, such as the OWASP Top Ten or the Microsoft Secure Development Lifecycle (SDL) guidelines. These policies can block code changes that don't meet security criteria, ensuring that security is part of your development process.

Incorporating these secure development practices into your Azure DevOps pipelines helps you build more resilient and secure applications. Security should not be an afterthought but an integral part of your DevOps culture, and Azure DevOps provides the tools and integrations to make that possible.

10.3. Azure Key Vault and Secrets Management

Managing secrets, keys, and certificates is a critical aspect of securing applications and infrastructure in Azure DevOps. Azure Key Vault is a fully managed service that helps you safeguard cryptographic keys and other secrets. In this section, we'll explore how Azure Key Vault can be integrated into your Azure DevOps pipelines for effective secrets management.

Key Vault Integration

Azure DevOps provides seamless integration with Azure Key Vault, allowing you to securely store and retrieve sensitive information, such as connection strings, API keys, and passwords. By using Key Vault, you can centralize the management of secrets and restrict access to authorized users and applications.

To integrate Key Vault into your Azure DevOps pipelines, you can use service connections and Azure DevOps variable groups. Service connections enable secure communication between your pipelines and Key Vault, while variable groups allow you to reference secrets stored in Key Vault directly in your pipeline tasks.

Here's an example of how to use a variable group with Key Vault secrets in an Azure DevOps YAML pipeline:

```
variables:
```

```
- group: my-keyvault-variable-group
```

In this example, my-keyvault-variable-group is a variable group that references secrets from Azure Key Vault. You can then use these variables in your pipeline tasks without exposing sensitive information in your pipeline definition.

Secret Rotation

Secret rotation is a fundamental security practice to mitigate the risk of unauthorized access due to compromised secrets. Azure Key Vault simplifies secret rotation by allowing you to periodically update secrets and certificates without requiring changes to your application code.

Automating secret rotation in Azure DevOps pipelines ensures that your applications always use up-to-date secrets without manual intervention. You can schedule pipeline runs to update secrets in Key Vault, and Azure DevOps variables will automatically reflect the latest values.

Audit and Monitoring

Azure Key Vault provides comprehensive auditing and monitoring capabilities to track access and usage of secrets and keys. You can enable auditing and diagnostics in Key Vault to generate logs and metrics that capture all relevant activities.

By integrating Azure Monitor and Log Analytics with Key Vault, you can gain insights into security events, identify potential threats, and proactively respond to security incidents. Azure DevOps pipelines can be configured to trigger alerts based on specific security events or anomalies detected in Key Vault.

Role-Based Access Control (RBAC)

Azure Key Vault uses Azure Active Directory (Azure AD) for authentication and authorization. You can define fine-grained access control policies to grant specific permissions to users and applications. Azure DevOps service connections can be configured with RBAC roles to ensure that only authorized entities can access Key Vault secrets.

For example, you can grant read-only access to a pipeline for retrieving secrets but restrict the ability to modify or delete secrets. This principle of least privilege helps enhance the security of your secrets management process.

Incorporating Azure Key Vault into your Azure DevOps pipelines strengthens the security of your applications by centralizing secrets management, automating rotation, and providing robust auditing and access control mechanisms. By following best practices for secrets management, you can reduce the risk of data breaches and security incidents.

10.4. Compliance and Governance in Azure DevOps

Ensuring compliance and governance in Azure DevOps is essential for organizations to meet regulatory requirements, enforce security policies, and maintain control over their DevOps processes. In this section, we'll explore the key considerations and strategies for achieving compliance and governance in Azure DevOps.

Regulatory Compliance

Many industries and regions have specific regulatory requirements related to software development and data handling. Azure DevOps provides a framework to help organizations comply with these regulations. Common regulatory standards include GDPR (General Data Protection Regulation), HIPAA (Health Insurance Portability and Accountability Act), and SOC 2 (Service Organization Control 2).

To achieve regulatory compliance, organizations can implement the following practices:

1. **Data Classification**: Identify and classify sensitive data within your DevOps pipelines and repositories. Use tools like Azure Information Protection to automatically label and protect sensitive information.
2. **Access Control**: Implement role-based access control (RBAC) to restrict access to DevOps resources based on job roles and responsibilities. Ensure that only authorized personnel can perform critical actions.
3. **Audit Trails**: Enable auditing and logging in Azure DevOps to track changes, access, and activities. Regularly review and analyze audit logs to identify potential security incidents or compliance violations.
4. **Encryption**: Use encryption techniques to protect data at rest and in transit. Azure DevOps and Azure services offer encryption options to safeguard sensitive information.
5. **Compliance Policies**: Define and enforce compliance policies using Azure Policy and Azure Blueprints. These tools allow you to automate the assessment and remediation of non-compliant resources.

Security and Identity Management

Effective security practices are vital for compliance and governance. Azure DevOps leverages Azure Active Directory (Azure AD) for identity management and authentication. To enhance security:

1. **Multi-Factor Authentication (MFA)**: Enforce MFA for Azure DevOps and Azure AD accounts to add an extra layer of security.
2. **Conditional Access**: Configure conditional access policies to control access based on specific conditions, such as location or device.
3. **Service Connections**: Securely manage service connections to external services like Azure Key Vault, ensuring that sensitive credentials are protected.
4. **Secrets Management**: As discussed in the previous section (10.3), integrate Azure Key Vault to securely manage secrets, keys, and certificates.

Compliance as Code

Implementing compliance as code allows you to define and enforce compliance policies using code and automation. Azure Policy, for example, enables you to define policy rules as code, which can be applied across your Azure resources, including those used by Azure DevOps.

By codifying compliance requirements, you can automatically evaluate and remediate non-compliant resources during the deployment pipeline. This approach ensures that compliance is maintained throughout the software development lifecycle.

Continuous Compliance Monitoring

Continuous monitoring is essential for identifying and addressing compliance issues in real-time. Azure DevOps integrates with Azure Monitor and Log Analytics to provide continuous monitoring and alerting capabilities. Organizations can set up alerts and notifications based on specific compliance-related events or anomalies.

Additionally, organizations can leverage Azure Security Center to gain visibility into the security posture of Azure DevOps resources and receive recommendations for improving security and compliance.

Third-Party Audits

In some cases, organizations may require third-party audits and certifications to validate compliance with specific regulations. Azure DevOps and Azure services are designed to support third-party audits by providing detailed audit logs, reports, and evidence of compliance.

By following these strategies and best practices, organizations can establish a robust compliance and governance framework within Azure DevOps. This ensures that software development processes adhere to regulatory requirements while maintaining security and control over DevOps activities.

10.5. Security Scanning and Threat Mitigation

Security scanning and threat mitigation are critical aspects of any Azure DevOps environment. Detecting vulnerabilities and addressing security threats early in the development lifecycle is essential to ensure the integrity and security of your applications. In this section, we'll explore various security scanning techniques and strategies for threat mitigation within Azure DevOps.

Static Application Security Testing (SAST)

Static Application Security Testing, or SAST, is a technique used to analyze the source code or binary code of an application for security vulnerabilities. Azure DevOps offers integrations with SAST tools like SonarQube and Checkmarx. These tools automatically scan your codebase for issues such as code injection, authentication weaknesses, and SQL injection.

To implement SAST in Azure DevOps:

1. **Integration**: Integrate your chosen SAST tool into your DevOps pipeline. This can be done through extensions or custom tasks.
2. **Automated Scanning**: Configure the pipeline to trigger SAST scans as part of your build process.
3. **Quality Gates**: Set up quality gates to fail the build or deployment if critical security issues are detected.

Dynamic Application Security Testing (DAST)

Dynamic Application Security Testing, or DAST, involves testing a running application for vulnerabilities. DAST tools simulate attacks and assess how the application responds. Azure DevOps can integrate with DAST tools like OWASP ZAP and Burp Suite.

To implement DAST in Azure DevOps:

1. **DAST Tools Integration**: Set up your DAST tool and configure it to target your application's URLs.
2. **Automated Testing**: Create a pipeline job to run

automated DAST tests against your application.
3. **Thresholds**: Define thresholds for acceptable vulnerability levels. Fail the build or deployment if thresholds are exceeded.

Dependency Scanning

Managing dependencies is crucial for security. Vulnerabilities in open-source libraries can pose significant risks. Azure DevOps integrates with dependency scanning tools like WhiteSource and Snyk.

To implement dependency scanning:

1. **Dependency Scanning Tools**: Integrate your chosen dependency scanning tool into your pipeline.
2. **Automated Scans**: Schedule automated scans to detect vulnerabilities in your project's dependencies.
3. **Policy Enforcement**: Set policies to automatically reject or quarantine packages with known vulnerabilities.

Container Security

For applications using containers, container security is paramount. Azure DevOps can be used in conjunction with container scanning tools like Aqua Security and Twistlock to assess the security of container images.

To ensure container security:

1. **Image Scanning**: Configure your CI/CD pipeline to scan container images for vulnerabilities before deployment.
2. **Immutable Infrastructure**: Implement immutable infrastructure practices to replace compromised containers

with updated, secure ones.

3. **Runtime Protection**: Utilize runtime security solutions to monitor and protect containers in production.

Threat Mitigation Strategies

In addition to scanning, threat mitigation strategies are essential:

1. **Patch Management**: Regularly update and patch all software components to address known vulnerabilities.
2. **Incident Response**: Develop an incident response plan to quickly address and mitigate security incidents.
3. **Security Training**: Provide security training to your development and operations teams to promote security awareness.
4. **Security Champions**: Appoint security champions within your teams to advocate for security best practices.
5. **Least Privilege**: Implement the principle of least privilege to restrict access and limit potential damage in case of a breach.
6. **Secure Coding Practices**: Enforce secure coding practices to prevent common vulnerabilities.
7. **Security Automation**: Automate security checks and threat responses wherever possible to reduce manual errors.

By integrating security scanning and following threat mitigation strategies, you can significantly enhance the security posture of your Azure DevOps environment. Continuously monitoring and addressing security threats will help protect your applications and data from potential breaches and vulnerabilities.

Chapter 11: Customizing and Extending Azure DevOps

11.1. Azure DevOps API Overview

Azure DevOps provides a powerful and flexible platform for software development and DevOps practices. One of the key strengths of Azure DevOps is its extensibility through APIs (Application Programming Interfaces). These APIs allow you to customize and automate various aspects of Azure DevOps to suit your organization's specific needs. In this section, we will explore the Azure DevOps API and how it can be leveraged to enhance your development and DevOps workflows.

Understanding Azure DevOps APIs

Azure DevOps offers a set of REST APIs that cover various services within the platform, including Azure Boards, Azure Repos, Azure Pipelines, and more. These APIs provide programmatic access to the data and functionality of Azure DevOps services. You can use these APIs to create, read, update, and delete resources such as work items, build definitions, release pipelines, and repositories.

The Azure DevOps API is based on industry-standard REST principles, making it accessible from a wide range of programming languages and tools. You can interact with the API using HTTP requests, and the responses are typically returned in JSON format, which is easy to parse and work with in most programming languages.

Authentication and Authorization

To access the Azure DevOps API, you need to authenticate your requests. Azure DevOps supports several authentication methods, including Personal Access Tokens (PATs), OAuth, and Azure Active Directory (Azure AD) authentication. PATs are a common choice for automation scenarios, as they can be easily generated and managed.

Additionally, Azure DevOps provides fine-grained access control through its role-based permissions system. You can assign users and groups specific roles and permissions at the project, repository, or organization level, ensuring that only authorized individuals or applications can perform specific actions via the API.

Use Cases for Azure DevOps API

The Azure DevOps API can be used for a wide range of customization and automation tasks. Some common use cases include:

1. **Work Item Automation**: You can create scripts or applications that automatically create, update, or query work items in Azure Boards based on specific events or criteria.
2. **Build and Release Pipeline Automation**: Automate the creation and management of build and release pipelines, including the configuration of build and deployment tasks.
3. **Integration with External Systems**: Integrate Azure DevOps with other tools and systems used in your organization, such as issue tracking systems, monitoring solutions, or custom dashboards.
4. **Reporting and Analytics**: Retrieve data from Azure DevOps to generate custom reports and dashboards

tailored to your organization's needs.

5. **Custom Extensions**: Develop and deploy custom extensions, widgets, and service hooks to extend the functionality of Azure DevOps and integrate it with third-party services.

Getting Started with Azure DevOps API

To get started with the Azure DevOps API, you'll need to:

1. **Generate a Personal Access Token (PAT)**: Create a PAT in Azure DevOps with the necessary permissions for your tasks. Keep this token secure and use it for authentication.
2. **Choose a Programming Language**: Select a programming language or tool that you are comfortable with and that supports making HTTP requests.
3. **Authenticate**: Use your PAT or other authentication methods to authenticate your requests to the API.
4. **Explore the API Documentation**: Refer to the official Azure DevOps REST API documentation for detailed information on available endpoints, request parameters, and response formats.
5. **Start Building**: Begin building scripts or applications to interact with Azure DevOps services programmatically.

In the subsequent sections of this chapter, we will delve deeper into specific use cases, code examples, and best practices for leveraging the Azure DevOps API to customize and extend your Azure DevOps environment.

11.2. Developing Custom Extensions

Custom extensions in Azure DevOps are a powerful way to enhance and tailor the platform to meet your specific requirements. These extensions can include custom widgets, service hooks, and integration points with third-party tools and services. In this section, we will explore how to develop custom extensions for Azure DevOps.

Overview of Custom Extensions

Custom extensions allow you to extend the functionality of Azure DevOps in various ways:

1. **Widgets**: You can create custom widgets that display specific information, charts, or data on your Azure DevOps dashboards. These widgets can be used to provide team members with quick access to relevant information or metrics.
2. **Service Hooks**: Service hooks enable you to trigger external actions or notifications based on events that occur within Azure DevOps. For example, you can set up a service hook to trigger a build in response to a code commit.
3. **Task Extensions**: Task extensions can be added to your build and release pipelines, providing additional functionality. You can create custom tasks to perform specific actions during the build or release process.
4. **Integration with Third-Party Services**: Custom extensions allow you to integrate Azure DevOps with other tools and services used in your development and DevOps workflows. This can include integrating with issue tracking systems, monitoring solutions, or deployment

tools.

Developing Custom Widgets

Custom widgets are a popular way to provide teams with tailored views of information within Azure DevOps. To develop custom widgets, you can use the Azure DevOps Web Extensions SDK, which provides the necessary tools and libraries for widget development. Here are the key steps to develop a custom widget:

1. **Set Up Your Development Environment**: Ensure you have Node.js and npm (Node Package Manager) installed. You'll also need the Azure DevOps Extension Generator to scaffold a new widget project.
2. **Create a New Widget Project**: Use the Extension Generator to create a new widget project. You'll be prompted to provide details such as the widget name, description, and layout.
3. **Customize the Widget**: Develop the widget logic using HTML, JavaScript, and CSS. You can use popular JavaScript frameworks such as React or Angular for building the user interface.
4. **Test Locally**: You can test your widget locally by running it in a development server. This allows you to see how the widget will appear and function within Azure DevOps.
5. **Package and Publish**: Once your widget is complete, package it as a .vsix (Visual Studio Extension) file and publish it to the Visual Studio Marketplace. This makes it available for installation in your Azure DevOps organization.

Creating Service Hooks

Service hooks are valuable for automating actions triggered by events in Azure DevOps. To create a custom service hook, you can use Azure Functions or any serverless platform to handle incoming webhook requests. Here are the steps to create a custom service hook:

1. **Create an Azure Function**: Set up an Azure Function that will receive webhook requests from Azure DevOps.
2. **Define the Webhook Payload**: Determine the payload structure that Azure DevOps will send to your function. This payload will contain information about the event that triggered the service hook.
3. **Handle Webhook Requests**: In your Azure Function, parse the incoming webhook request and implement the logic to perform the desired action based on the event data.
4. **Register the Service Hook**: In Azure DevOps, navigate to the project settings and configure a new service hook that points to your Azure Function URL.
5. **Test and Monitor**: Test your service hook by triggering events within Azure DevOps. Monitor the logs and behavior of your Azure Function to ensure it's working correctly.

Integrating Third-Party Tools

Custom extensions can also facilitate integration with third-party tools and services. Depending on the specific integration requirements, you may need to develop custom connectors or scripts to interact with external APIs. Popular integration scenarios include connecting Azure DevOps with issue trackers, chat platforms, and continuous integration/continuous deployment (CI/CD) tools.

In the subsequent sections of this chapter, we will provide code examples and practical guidance for developing custom extensions in Azure DevOps. Whether you're building custom widgets, service hooks, or integrations, custom extensions can significantly enhance your Azure DevOps environment and streamline your development workflows.

11.3. Automating Tasks with Azure CLI and PowerShell

Automation is a key aspect of Azure DevOps, allowing you to streamline repetitive tasks and ensure consistency in your development and deployment processes. Azure DevOps provides support for automation through various scripting languages, with Azure CLI (Command Line Interface) and PowerShell being two popular choices. In this section, we will explore how you can use Azure CLI and PowerShell for automating tasks in Azure DevOps.

Using Azure CLI for Automation

Azure CLI is a command-line tool provided by Microsoft for managing Azure resources. It enables you to automate various Azure-related tasks, such as creating virtual machines, managing storage accounts, and configuring Azure services. Here are some common use cases for using Azure CLI in Azure DevOps:

1. **Resource Provisioning**: You can use Azure CLI to create and manage Azure resources, such as virtual machines, databases, and storage accounts. This is especially useful for provisioning resources as part of your deployment pipelines.
2. **Azure Resource Management**: Azure CLI allows you to interact with Azure Resource Manager, enabling you to

deploy and manage templates for Azure resources. This is commonly used for infrastructure as code (IaC) scenarios.

3. **Azure DevOps Service Management**: Azure DevOps itself can be managed and configured using Azure CLI. You can automate the setup of projects, repositories, and service connections.
4. **Azure DevOps Extension Management**: Azure CLI also provides commands for managing Azure DevOps extensions. You can use these commands to install, update, or uninstall extensions as needed.

To use Azure CLI in your Azure DevOps pipelines, you can add a script task and select the appropriate Azure CLI version. You can then write Azure CLI commands directly in the script task to automate your desired tasks.

Leveraging PowerShell for Automation

PowerShell is a versatile scripting language and automation framework that is widely used in Windows environments. Azure DevOps fully supports PowerShell, allowing you to automate tasks across various stages of your development and deployment processes. Here are some common scenarios where PowerShell automation is valuable:

1. **Azure Resource Management**: PowerShell provides Azure modules that allow you to manage Azure resources, similar to Azure CLI. You can create, update, and delete Azure resources using PowerShell scripts.
2. **Azure DevOps Task Automation**: PowerShell scripts can be used in Azure DevOps pipelines as custom tasks. You can write scripts to build, test, deploy, and configure your applications and services.

3. **Azure DevOps Administration**: PowerShell can be used for Azure DevOps administration tasks, such as managing users, permissions, and security settings within your Azure DevOps organization.
4. **Integration with External Systems**: PowerShell can also be used to interact with external systems and services. You can write scripts to integrate Azure DevOps with third-party tools and automate data transfer or synchronization.

To use PowerShell in your Azure DevOps pipelines, you can add a PowerShell task and specify the script or script file you want to execute. PowerShell scripts can be run on hosted agents, ensuring that your automation tasks are executed in a controlled and isolated environment.

In the upcoming sections, we will provide examples and best practices for using Azure CLI and PowerShell for automation in Azure DevOps. Whether you prefer Azure CLI's simplicity or PowerShell's scripting capabilities, both options empower you to automate and streamline your DevOps workflows effectively.

11.4. Integration with Third-Party Tools

In modern DevOps practices, integration with third-party tools plays a crucial role in extending the capabilities of Azure DevOps and streamlining your workflows. Azure DevOps provides various ways to integrate with external systems and tools, allowing you to leverage existing solutions and enhance your automation processes. In this section, we will explore the importance of third-party tool integration in Azure DevOps and provide insights into how you can achieve seamless integration.

The Significance of Third-Party Tool Integration

Third-party tools are essential for addressing specific requirements and enhancing the functionality of your DevOps pipelines. These tools cover a wide range of areas, including monitoring, security, testing, deployment, and collaboration. Here are some reasons why integrating third-party tools is vital:

1. **Specialized Capabilities**: Third-party tools often offer specialized features and capabilities that might not be available in Azure DevOps natively. Integrating these tools allows you to leverage their strengths.
2. **Enhanced Security**: Security tools and services can help you identify vulnerabilities and threats in your applications and infrastructure. Integrating security solutions into your pipelines helps ensure the security of your deployments.
3. **Compliance and Governance**: Many organizations have specific compliance and governance requirements. Third-party tools can assist in enforcing these policies and reporting on compliance.
4. **Customization**: Third-party tools can be customized to fit your unique workflow and requirements. Integration allows you to tailor these tools to your specific needs.

Integration Approaches

Azure DevOps offers several approaches for integrating with third-party tools:

1. **Service Hooks**: Azure DevOps Service Hooks enable you to connect your pipelines and Azure DevOps events to external services. You can use these hooks to trigger actions in third-party tools based on events like code commits, work item changes, or build completions.

2. **APIs**: Azure DevOps provides a rich set of REST APIs that allow you to programmatically interact with your Azure DevOps organization. You can use these APIs to retrieve data, create work items, manage pipelines, and more. This makes it possible to build custom integrations with third-party systems.
3. **Extensions**: Azure DevOps Marketplace offers a wide range of extensions and integrations with third-party tools. You can search for extensions that suit your needs and install them in your Azure DevOps organization.
4. **Custom Scripts**: For more advanced integrations, you can use custom scripts and automation. PowerShell, Azure CLI, and other scripting languages can be employed to connect Azure DevOps with external systems and perform tasks like data synchronization or custom deployments.

Examples of Third-Party Tool Integration

1. **JIRA Integration**: Many organizations use JIRA for issue tracking and project management. Azure DevOps allows you to integrate with JIRA, enabling you to create, update, and link work items between the two systems. This ensures seamless collaboration between development and other teams using JIRA.
2. **Slack Integration**: Integrating Azure DevOps with Slack allows you to receive real-time notifications and updates in your Slack channels. You can set up alerts for build failures, work item changes, or other critical events, keeping your team informed.
3. **SonarQube Integration**: SonarQube is a popular code quality and security analysis tool. Integrating SonarQube with Azure DevOps enables you to perform code analysis as part of your build and release pipelines, ensuring code

quality and security compliance.

4. **GitHub Integration**: If you host your source code in GitHub, you can integrate it seamlessly with Azure DevOps. This allows you to trigger Azure DevOps builds and releases whenever code changes are pushed to GitHub repositories.
5. **Docker Integration**: If your application relies on containerization, you can integrate Azure DevOps with Docker Hub or other container registries. This ensures that your Docker images are built, stored, and deployed efficiently as part of your CI/CD process.

In the next section, we will explore real-world case studies of custom solutions and integrations with third-party tools to demonstrate the flexibility and power of Azure DevOps in meeting diverse DevOps requirements.

11.5. Case Studies: Custom Solutions in Azure DevOps

In this section, we will explore real-world case studies of custom solutions built using Azure DevOps. These case studies demonstrate how organizations have leveraged Azure DevOps to address unique challenges and optimize their DevOps workflows. Custom solutions often involve using Azure DevOps APIs, custom extensions, and automation scripts to tailor the platform to specific needs.

Case Study 1: Release Pipeline Orchestration

Challenge: A large e-commerce company needed to streamline the release process for its complex microservices-based application. The existing release pipelines were manual and error-prone, leading to deployment issues and delays.

Solution: The organization implemented a custom solution using Azure DevOps REST APIs and PowerShell scripts. They created a release pipeline orchestration system that automatically detected code changes, triggered appropriate build pipelines, and orchestrated the deployment of microservices in the correct order.

Results: The custom solution reduced deployment errors by 90% and significantly accelerated the release cycle. It also improved visibility into the release process, allowing teams to track the status of each microservice deployment in real-time.

Case Study 2: Compliance Reporting

Challenge: A financial institution needed to ensure compliance with strict regulatory requirements. They were required to provide detailed reports on every code change, work item modification, and build and release pipeline execution.

Solution: The organization built a custom compliance reporting system using Azure DevOps APIs and Power BI. They created automated workflows that collected data from Azure DevOps, generated compliance reports, and stored them securely for auditing purposes.

Results: The custom solution not only ensured compliance but also reduced the manual effort required for reporting by 80%. Auditors could quickly access historical data and reports, making the compliance process more efficient.

Case Study 3: Cross-Platform Testing

Challenge: A software development company needed to perform extensive cross-platform testing for its mobile application, which ran on both iOS and Android devices. Managing multiple testing environments and devices was time-consuming and error-prone.

Solution: The organization used Azure DevOps to create a custom cross-platform testing solution. They leveraged Azure DevTest Labs to automate the provisioning of test environments and integrated with popular mobile testing frameworks. This allowed them to run tests simultaneously on various devices and operating systems.

Results: The custom testing solution reduced testing time by 60% and improved test coverage. Developers could identify and fix issues more quickly, leading to a more reliable and stable mobile application.

Case Study 4: Security Scanning and Vulnerability Management

Challenge: A cybersecurity firm needed to ensure the security of its software products. They wanted to integrate security scanning tools into their CI/CD pipelines to identify vulnerabilities and weaknesses in their code.

Solution: The organization integrated security scanning tools, such as SonarQube and OWASP ZAP, into their Azure DevOps pipelines. Custom scripts were used to automate code analysis, vulnerability scanning, and security testing as part of the deployment process.

Results: The custom solution helped identify and mitigate security vulnerabilities early in the development cycle. It improved the overall security posture of their software products and reduced the risk of security breaches.

These case studies highlight the versatility of Azure DevOps in addressing diverse challenges across different industries. Custom solutions and integrations empower organizations to tailor their DevOps practices to meet specific requirements, enhance efficiency, and achieve better outcomes. Whether it's automating release pipelines, ensuring compliance, streamlining testing, or enhancing security, Azure DevOps offers the flexibility and extensibility needed to succeed in the world of DevOps.

12.1. Cloud Environment Basics

In this section, we will delve into the fundamentals of cloud environments and their significance within the context of Azure DevOps. Cloud computing has revolutionized the way organizations manage their IT resources and execute software development projects. Understanding the basics of cloud environments is crucial for successfully integrating cloud services into your DevOps practices.

What Is a Cloud Environment?

A cloud environment, often referred to as a cloud computing environment, is a virtualized infrastructure that provides on-demand access to a wide range of computing resources over the internet. These resources can include virtual machines, storage, databases, networking components, and various application services. Cloud environments are hosted and maintained by cloud service providers like Microsoft Azure, Amazon Web Services (AWS), and Google Cloud Platform (GCP).

Key Characteristics of Cloud Environments

Cloud environments exhibit several key characteristics that differentiate them from traditional on-premises infrastructure:

1. **On-Demand Self-Service**: Users can provision and

manage cloud resources as needed, without requiring human intervention from the service provider.

2. **Scalability and Elasticity**: Cloud resources can be easily scaled up or down to accommodate changes in workload or demand. This ensures efficient resource utilization and cost optimization.
3. **Resource Pooling**: Cloud providers pool computing resources to serve multiple customers. Resources are dynamically allocated and reassigned based on demand.
4. **Rapid Elasticity**: Cloud resources can be provisioned and decommissioned quickly in response to changes in demand, allowing for agility and flexibility in resource allocation.
5. **Broad Network Access**: Cloud services are accessible over the internet from a variety of devices, promoting accessibility and collaboration.
6. **Measured Service**: Cloud usage is metered and billed based on actual resource consumption, enabling cost control and transparency.

Types of Cloud Environments

There are different deployment models for cloud environments, each offering a distinct set of advantages and use cases:

1. **Public Cloud**: Public cloud environments are owned and operated by third-party cloud service providers. They are open to the public and offer resources on a pay-as-you-go basis. Examples include Microsoft Azure, AWS, and GCP.
2. **Private Cloud**: Private cloud environments are dedicated to a single organization and can be hosted on-premises or by a third-party provider. They offer greater control, security, and customization but require more significant

upfront investments.

3. **Hybrid Cloud**: Hybrid cloud environments combine both public and private cloud resources, allowing data and applications to be shared between them. This model provides flexibility and can help bridge the gap between existing on-premises infrastructure and the cloud.

Benefits of Cloud Environments in DevOps

Integrating cloud environments into your DevOps practices offers several benefits:

- **Scalability**: Easily scale infrastructure resources up or down to meet changing demands, supporting continuous integration and delivery.

- **Cost Efficiency**: Pay only for the resources you use, reducing capital expenditures and optimizing costs.

- **Flexibility**: Quickly provision and test new environments, speeding up development and testing processes.

- **Global Reach**: Access cloud resources from anywhere in the world, promoting collaboration in distributed teams.

- **Security**: Cloud providers offer robust security features and compliance certifications to enhance data protection.

- **Disaster Recovery**: Implement automated disaster recovery plans in the cloud to ensure business continuity.

In summary, understanding the basics of cloud environments is crucial for modern DevOps practices. Cloud computing provides the infrastructure backbone for agile development, scalability, and cost-efficiency. In the subsequent sections of this chapter, we will explore how Azure DevOps can be integrated with cloud environments to effectively manage and deploy cloud-based services and applications.

12.2. Deploying and Managing Azure Services

In this section, we will dive into the process of deploying and managing Azure services within your Azure DevOps environment. Microsoft Azure offers a wide range of cloud services, including virtual machines, databases, web applications, and more. Understanding how to provision and manage these services is crucial for effectively utilizing the cloud in your DevOps workflows.

Azure Resource Groups

Before we start deploying Azure services, it's essential to grasp the concept of Azure Resource Groups. An Azure Resource Group is a logical container that holds related Azure resources. These resources can be Azure virtual machines, databases, storage accounts, and more. Resource Groups are useful for organizing resources, managing access control, and monitoring usage.

When working with Azure DevOps, you can create and manage Azure Resource Groups directly from your DevOps pipelines. This allows you to automate the creation of resource groups and their associated resources as part of your deployment process.

Deploying Azure Services with Azure DevOps

Azure DevOps provides various tools and services to deploy Azure resources. Two primary methods include:

1. **Azure Resource Manager (ARM) Templates**: ARM templates are JSON files that define the resources you need to deploy. You can create, modify, and deploy these templates using Azure DevOps pipelines. ARM templates enable infrastructure as code (IaC) and provide version control for your infrastructure.
2. **Azure DevTest Labs**: Azure DevTest Labs is a service that allows you to create and manage virtual machines for development and testing purposes. You can use Azure DevOps to automate the creation and deletion of lab environments, saving time and resources.

Here is a simplified example of an ARM template for deploying an Azure virtual machine:

```
{

"$schema": "https://schema.management.azure.com/schemas/2019-04-01/deploymentTemplate.json#",

"contentVersion": "1.0.0.0",

"resources": [

{

"type": "Microsoft.Compute/virtualMachines",

"apiVersion": "2020-12-01",

"name": "myVM",
```

```
"location": "[resourceGroup().location]",
"properties": {
"hardwareProfile": {
"vmSize": "Standard_DS2_v2"
},
"osProfile": {
"computerName": "myVM",
"adminUsername": "adminUser",
"adminPassword": "yourPassword"
},
"storageProfile": {
"imageReference": {
"publisher": "MicrosoftWindowsServer",
"offer": "WindowsServer",
"sku": "2019-Datacenter",
"version": "latest"
},
"osDisk": {
"createOption": "FromImage"
}
```

```
},
"networkProfile": {
"networkInterfaces": [
{
"id": "[resourceId('Microsoft.Network/networkInterfaces', 'myNIC')]"
}
]
}
}
}
]
}
```

This example ARM template deploys a Windows virtual machine (VM) in Azure.

Managing Azure Resources

Once you've deployed Azure services, it's crucial to manage and monitor them effectively. Azure DevOps offers integration with Azure Monitor and Log Analytics, which allows you to:

- Collect and analyze telemetry data from your Azure resources.

- Set up alerts and notifications based on specific conditions.
- Gain insights into resource performance and usage.
- Monitor the health and availability of your applications.

Azure DevOps pipelines can be configured to trigger based on specific events, such as resource changes or alerts, ensuring that your deployment and management processes remain automated and responsive.

In summary, deploying and managing Azure services within your Azure DevOps workflows is a fundamental aspect of modern DevOps practices. It allows you to leverage the scalability and flexibility of the cloud while maintaining control and visibility over your cloud resources. The next section will explore how to integrate cloud and on-premises environments effectively for seamless DevOps operations.

12.3. Integrating Cloud and On-Premises Environments

In this section, we'll explore the integration of cloud and on-premises environments within the context of Azure DevOps. Modern organizations often have a mix of cloud-based resources and on-premises infrastructure. Integrating these environments seamlessly is crucial for achieving end-to-end DevOps automation and managing hybrid solutions effectively.

Azure Hybrid Connections

Azure provides a solution called Azure Hybrid Connections, which enables secure and easy integration between Azure resources and on-premises systems. These connections allow you to access on-premises services, such as databases or web services, from your Azure resources, including virtual machines, web apps, and Azure Functions.

To set up an Azure Hybrid Connection:

1. **Create a Hybrid Connection**: In the Azure portal, you can create a Hybrid Connection and specify the hostname and port of the on-premises service you want to access.
2. **Install the Hybrid Connection Manager**: On your on-premises server, install the Azure Hybrid Connection Manager. This manager acts as a bridge between your Azure resources and on-premises services.
3. **Configure the Connection**: In the Hybrid Connection Manager, configure the connection to use the previously created Hybrid Connection.
4. **Update Application Settings**: For Azure resources like web apps or Azure Functions, update the application settings to use the Hybrid Connection.

Here's an example of configuring an Azure Function to use a Hybrid Connection to access an on-premises SQL Server database:

```
using System;

using System.Data.SqlClient;

using Microsoft.Azure.WebJobs;

using Microsoft.Extensions.Configuration;

using Microsoft.Extensions.Logging;

public static class OnPremiseDatabaseFunction
```

```
{
[FunctionName("ProcessOnPremiseData")]
public static void Run(
[TimerTrigger("0 */5 * * * *")] TimerInfo myTimer,
ILogger log,
ExecutionContext context)
{
// Load configuration from Azure Functions application settings
var config = new ConfigurationBuilder()
.SetBasePath(context.FunctionAppDirectory)
.AddJsonFile("local.settings.json", optional: true, reloadOnChange: true)
.AddEnvironmentVariables()
.Build();
// Retrieve the connection string from application settings
string connectionString = config["OnPremiseDbConnection"];
// Use the connection string to connect to the on-premises SQL Server
using (SqlConnection connection = new SqlConnection(connectionString))
{
connection.Open();
```

```
// Perform database operations here
log.LogInformation("Connected to on-premises SQL Server.");
}
}
}
```

Azure Arc

Azure Arc is another powerful tool for managing hybrid environments. It extends Azure management and services to on-premises and multi-cloud environments, allowing you to use Azure management tools, such as Azure Policy and Azure Monitor, across all your resources.

With Azure Arc, you can:

- **Manage On-Premises Servers**: Register your on-premises servers with Azure Arc to centrally manage and monitor them.
- **Apply Azure Policies**: Enforce governance and compliance policies consistently across all environments, whether in Azure or on-premises.
- **Monitor and Secure Resources**: Use Azure Monitor and Azure Security Center to gain insights and enhance the security of your hybrid resources.
- **Deploy Azure Services Anywhere**: Extend Azure services like Azure Kubernetes Service (AKS) or Azure Functions to your on-premises or multi-cloud environments.

The integration of cloud and on-premises environments is essential for organizations with existing infrastructure investments. By leveraging Azure Hybrid Connections and Azure Arc, you can maintain a unified DevOps workflow while seamlessly managing resources across different environments.

In the next section, we will delve into cost management and optimization strategies for cloud resources, ensuring that you make the most of your Azure investments.

12.4. Cost Management and Optimization in the Cloud

Cost management and optimization are essential aspects of managing cloud resources effectively. In this section, we will explore strategies and best practices for controlling costs and ensuring that you make the most of your investments in the cloud.

1. Resource Tagging

One of the fundamental practices for cost management is resource tagging. Tags are key-value pairs that you can assign to your Azure resources. They provide metadata that helps you categorize, track, and allocate costs more effectively. By tagging resources with attributes like department, project, or environment, you gain better visibility into how resources are used.

Here's an example of how to apply tags to an Azure resource using Azure PowerShell:

```
# Assign tags to a resource group

Set-AzResourceGroup -Name "MyResourceGroup" -Tag @{ Department = "Finance"; Environment = "Production" }
```

 # Assign tags to a virtual machine

Set-AzVM -ResourceGroupName "MyResourceGroup" -Name "MyVM" -Tag @{ Project = "ProjectX"; Owner = "John Doe" }

2. Azure Cost Management and Billing

Azure provides a dedicated service called Azure Cost Management and Billing, which helps you monitor, analyze, and optimize your cloud spending. You can use this service to:

- **Track Spending**: Get a detailed view of your Azure spending, broken down by resource, subscription, or department.

- **Create Budgets**: Set spending limits and receive alerts when your spending approaches or exceeds those limits.

- **Analyze Costs**: Analyze cost trends, forecast future spending, and identify cost-saving opportunities.

- **Recommendations**: Receive recommendations on how to optimize your resources for cost savings.

3. Right-Sizing Resources

Right-sizing involves matching the size and performance of your cloud resources to your actual workload requirements. Over-provisioning or under-provisioning resources can lead to unnecessary costs. Azure provides tools like Azure Advisor and Azure Monitor to help you identify underutilized or overutilized resources.

4. Reserved Instances

Azure Reserved Virtual Machine Instances allow you to commit to using virtual machines for a one- or three-year term to reduce your overall computing costs. By reserving resources upfront, you can save up to 72% compared to pay-as-you-go pricing.

5. Serverless Computing

Consider using serverless computing services like Azure Functions or Azure Logic Apps. These services automatically scale based on demand, eliminating the need to provision and pay for idle resources.

6. Automation and Policies

Leverage automation and policies to enforce cost-saving measures. For example, you can schedule virtual machines to automatically shut down during non-business hours or enforce policies that prevent the creation of costly resource configurations.

7. Continuous Monitoring

Implement continuous monitoring of your cloud resources to detect cost anomalies or unexpected spikes in usage. Azure Monitor, along with custom alerts and dashboards, can help you stay informed about resource activity.

8. Cloud Governance

Establish clear governance practices within your organization to manage and control cloud spending effectively. Define roles and responsibilities for resource provisioning and cost management.

9. Review and Optimize

Regularly review your Azure spending, analyze cost reports, and make adjustments as needed. Optimization is an ongoing process that requires proactive management.

By following these cost management and optimization strategies, you can ensure that your Azure cloud resources are both cost-effective and aligned with your organization's needs. In the next section, we will explore disaster recovery and high availability strategies for cloud environments.

12.5. Disaster Recovery and High Availability Strategies

Disaster recovery (DR) and high availability (HA) are critical considerations when managing cloud environments in Azure. These strategies ensure that your services and data remain accessible and recoverable in the face of unexpected outages or disasters. In this section, we'll explore best practices for implementing DR and HA in Azure.

1. Understanding High Availability

High availability refers to the ability of a system or service to remain operational and accessible even in the presence of hardware or software failures. Azure provides several features and services that contribute to high availability:

- **Availability Sets**: Availability sets are logical groupings of virtual machines (VMs) that are placed across multiple physical servers. This configuration ensures that if a hardware failure occurs, not all VMs are affected simultaneously.

- **Load Balancers**: Azure Load Balancers distribute incoming network traffic across multiple healthy VM instances. This helps in distributing the load and ensuring that your application remains accessible even if some instances fail.

- **Azure App Service Environments**: Azure App Service Environments (ASE) offer isolated and highly scalable app runtimes. ASEs can be configured with multiple instances across different fault domains and update domains for high availability.

2. Implementing Disaster Recovery

Disaster recovery (DR) focuses on ensuring that your services and data can be quickly recovered after a disaster, such as a region-wide outage. Azure provides several tools and services for implementing DR:

- **Azure Site Recovery**: Azure Site Recovery is a service that helps you replicate workloads running on physical and virtual machines (VMs) from a primary site to a secondary location. This secondary location can be in a different Azure region or an on-premises datacenter. In the event of a disaster, you can fail over to the secondary location to minimize downtime.

- **Geo-Redundant Storage (GRS)**: Azure Storage offers GRS, which replicates your data to a secondary Azure region. This provides data redundancy and availability in case of a regional outage.

- **Azure Backup**: Azure Backup allows you to regularly back up your virtual machines, files, and databases. You can store backups in a different Azure region for added redundancy.

- **Traffic Manager**: Azure Traffic Manager allows you to distribute incoming traffic across multiple Azure regions. In the event of a regional outage, traffic can be automatically redirected to a healthy region.

3. Testing and Validation

Implementing DR and HA strategies is not enough; you must regularly test and validate your configurations. Conducting planned failovers and performing disaster recovery drills helps ensure that your recovery procedures work as expected.

4. Monitoring and Alerting

Utilize Azure Monitor and Azure Security Center to monitor the health and security of your cloud resources. Set up alerts to notify you of any critical events, such as resource failures or security breaches.

5. Documentation and Runbooks

Document your DR and HA procedures in detail, and create runbooks that outline step-by-step instructions for executing failovers or recovery processes. Well-documented procedures are essential during high-stress situations.

6. Compliance and Regulation

Consider regulatory requirements and compliance standards when designing your DR and HA strategies. Ensure that your disaster recovery plans align with these standards and include data encryption and protection measures.

7. Regular Reviews and Updates

Regularly review and update your DR and HA plans to account for changes in your infrastructure, applications, and business requirements. Cloud environments are dynamic, and your strategies should adapt accordingly.

By implementing high availability and disaster recovery strategies in Azure, you can minimize downtime, protect your data, and ensure business continuity, even in the face of unexpected disruptions. In the next chapter, we will delve into the importance of building a DevOps culture and best practices for fostering it within your organization.

Chapter 13: DevOps Culture and Best Practices

13.1. Building a DevOps Culture

A DevOps culture is at the heart of successful DevOps adoption within an organization. It's not just about adopting tools and practices; it's about fostering a mindset and culture of collaboration, communication, and continuous improvement. In this section, we'll explore the key aspects of building a DevOps culture.

1. Collaboration and Communication

DevOps emphasizes breaking down silos between development, operations, and other teams involved in the software delivery process. Encourage open and transparent communication between these teams. This can be achieved through regular meetings, shared tools, and collaboration platforms like Microsoft Teams and Slack.

2. Shared Goals and Objectives

Ensure that all teams share common goals and objectives related to software quality, delivery speed, and customer satisfaction. Alignment on these goals promotes a sense of ownership and accountability among team members.

3. Automation and Infrastructure as Code (IaC)

Implement automation as a core principle of your DevOps culture. Infrastructure as Code (IaC) allows you to define and manage infrastructure using code, ensuring consistency and repeatability. Tools like Azure Resource Manager (ARM) templates and Terraform can help in this regard.

4. Continuous Integration and Continuous Delivery (CI/CD)

Embrace CI/CD pipelines to automate the building, testing, and deployment of software. These pipelines enable faster and more reliable software releases. Azure Pipelines and Jenkins are popular tools for setting up CI/CD workflows.

5. Feedback Loops

Establish feedback loops at every stage of the software delivery process. Collect feedback from end-users, testers, and operations teams. Use this feedback to drive improvements and prioritize feature development.

6. Learning and Knowledge Sharing

Promote a culture of continuous learning and knowledge sharing. Encourage team members to acquire new skills and share their knowledge with others. This can include organizing lunch-and-learn sessions, workshops, and training programs.

7. Failure as a Learning Opportunity

Encourage a "blame-free" culture where failures are viewed as learning opportunities. When something goes wrong, focus on identifying the root cause and implementing preventive measures rather than assigning blame.

8. Cross-Functional Teams

Consider organizing teams around specific products or services rather than functional roles. Cross-functional teams can take ownership of end-to-end delivery, fostering collaboration and reducing handoffs.

9. Leadership Support

DevOps adoption requires support from leadership. Leaders should champion the cultural shift, provide resources, and set an example through their actions. They should also invest in tools and training to enable DevOps practices.

10. Measurement and Metrics

Define key performance indicators (KPIs) that align with your DevOps goals. Measure and track these metrics to assess the effectiveness of your DevOps culture and identify areas for improvement.

11. Continuous Improvement

DevOps is an ongoing journey of continuous improvement. Regularly assess your processes, tools, and culture. Solicit feedback from team members and stakeholders to identify areas where you can enhance your DevOps practices.

Building a DevOps culture is a fundamental step towards achieving the benefits of DevOps, including faster delivery, improved quality, and increased customer satisfaction. In the next sections, we'll explore strategies for overcoming common challenges in DevOps adoption and the importance of continuous learning and improvement.

13.2. Overcoming Common Challenges in DevOps Adoption

While DevOps brings numerous benefits to organizations, its adoption is not without challenges. Recognizing and addressing these challenges is crucial for a successful DevOps transformation.

In this section, we'll discuss some common obstacles that teams may encounter and strategies for overcoming them.

1. Resistance to Change

One of the most significant challenges in DevOps adoption is resistance to change. Team members, especially those accustomed to traditional workflows, may resist the cultural and process changes associated with DevOps. To address this challenge:

- **Communicate the Benefits:** Clearly communicate the benefits of DevOps, such as faster delivery, improved collaboration, and reduced manual work.

- **Provide Training:** Offer training and resources to help team members acquire the skills needed for DevOps practices.

- **Start Small:** Begin with small, manageable changes and gradually expand DevOps practices to build confidence.

2. Siloed Teams

In some organizations, teams work in silos, with little interaction between development, operations, and other groups. Silos can hinder collaboration and transparency. To break down silos:

- **Cross-Functional Teams:** Form cross-functional teams that take ownership of end-to-end delivery, fostering collaboration and shared responsibility.

- **Shared Tools:** Use collaboration tools like Microsoft Teams, Slack, and shared documentation platforms to facilitate communication.

3. Legacy Systems

Legacy systems with complex architectures and dependencies can pose challenges in DevOps adoption. These systems may require significant refactoring or modernization efforts. To address this:

- **Incremental Modernization:** Break down modernization efforts into smaller, incremental changes to avoid disruption.

- **Automated Testing:** Implement automated testing to ensure the stability of legacy systems during updates.

4. Tooling and Technology

Selecting the right DevOps tools and technologies can be daunting. Teams may struggle with tool integration and configuration. To navigate this challenge:

- **Tool Evaluation:** Evaluate tools based on your specific needs and requirements. Consider factors like ease of integration, scalability, and community support.

- **Consult Experts:** Seek guidance from experts or consult with vendors to ensure proper tool setup and configuration.

5. Security and Compliance

Security and compliance are paramount in DevOps, but they can sometimes slow down the delivery process. To balance security and speed:

- **Shift Left Security:** Integrate security practices earlier in the development lifecycle (shift-left) to identify and mitigate issues sooner.

- **Automation:** Implement security testing and compliance checks as part of your CI/CD pipelines.

6. Measuring Success

Measuring the success of your DevOps initiatives can be challenging without clear metrics. To measure and demonstrate success:

- **Define KPIs:** Define key performance indicators (KPIs) aligned with your DevOps goals, such as deployment frequency, lead time, and defect rate.

- **Regular Assessment:** Continuously assess your processes and tools to identify areas for improvement based on the defined KPIs.

7. Scaling DevOps

As organizations grow, scaling DevOps practices across multiple teams and projects can be complex. To scale effectively:

- **Standardize Practices:** Develop standardized DevOps practices and guidelines that teams can follow.

- **Centralized Support:** Provide centralized support and resources to assist teams in adopting DevOps.

Overcoming these challenges requires a combination of technical solutions and cultural changes. It's important to recognize that DevOps adoption is an ongoing journey, and organizations should remain flexible and open to continuous improvement. In the following sections, we'll explore the importance of continuous learning and improvement in DevOps and delve into leadership and change management practices.

13.3. Continuous Learning and Improvement in DevOps

Continuous learning and improvement are core principles of DevOps. In this section, we'll explore the importance of ongoing education and fostering a culture of improvement within DevOps teams.

1. The DevOps Learning Journey

DevOps is a dynamic field that evolves rapidly as new tools, technologies, and best practices emerge. DevOps professionals must embark on a continuous learning journey to stay up-to-date with the latest developments. This journey includes:

- **Exploration of New Tools:** DevOps practitioners should regularly evaluate and experiment with new tools and technologies that can enhance their workflows.

- **Skill Development:** Learning new skills, such as scripting, automation, and containerization, is essential for DevOps professionals.

- **Keeping Abreast of Industry Trends:** Staying informed about industry trends, conferences, and community events helps professionals gain valuable insights.

2. Learning Resources

To support continuous learning, a wealth of resources is available:

- **Online Courses and Tutorials:** Platforms like Coursera, Udemy, and Pluralsight offer a wide range of DevOps courses.

- **Blogs and Forums:** DevOps blogs and forums provide practical insights and solutions shared by the community.

- **Books and Documentation:** There are numerous books and official documentation for DevOps tools and practices.

- **Webinars and Conferences:** Attending webinars and conferences allows professionals to learn from experts and network with peers.

3. Cross-Functional Training

DevOps emphasizes collaboration between development and operations teams. Cross-functional training helps team members understand each other's roles and challenges. For example:

- **Developers Learning Operations:** Developers can benefit from understanding infrastructure as code (IaC) and system administration to create more deployable code.

- **Operations Learning Development:** Operations teams can gain insights into application development and coding practices to better support developers.

4. Fostering a Culture of Improvement

A culture of continuous improvement is fundamental to DevOps success. It involves:

- **Encouraging Feedback:** Teams should encourage open and honest feedback from all members to identify areas for improvement.

- **Retropectives:** Conducting regular retrospectives allows teams to reflect on their processes, celebrate successes, and address challenges.

- **Experimentation:** Teams should feel empowered to experiment with new ideas and technologies and learn from both successes and failures.

5. DevOps Metrics

Measuring the effectiveness of DevOps practices is crucial. Key performance indicators (KPIs) and metrics can include:

- **Deployment Frequency:** How often new code is deployed to production.

- **Lead Time:** The time it takes to move from code commit to deployment.

- **Change Failure Rate:** The percentage of deployments that result in failures.

- **Mean Time to Recovery (MTTR):** The time it takes to recover from failures or incidents.

These metrics provide insights into the efficiency and reliability of DevOps processes and help teams identify areas for improvement.

6. DevOps Certification

DevOps certification programs, such as Certified DevOps Engineer (CDE) or Certified Kubernetes Administrator (CKA), can validate skills and knowledge. While certification is not mandatory, it can be a valuable addition to a DevOps professional's resume.

In summary, continuous learning and improvement are at the core of DevOps. DevOps practitioners should embrace a mindset of lifelong learning, leverage available resources, and foster a culture of improvement within their teams. This commitment to growth and evolution is what sets DevOps apart as a transformative approach to software development and IT operations.

13.4. Leadership and Change Management in DevOps

Leadership and change management play a pivotal role in the successful adoption of DevOps practices within organizations. In this section, we will delve into the importance of leadership, strategies for leading DevOps initiatives, and effective change management approaches.

1. The Role of Leadership

Leadership is instrumental in driving cultural and process changes necessary for DevOps. Here are key aspects of leadership in a DevOps context:

- **Vision and Strategy:** Leaders must articulate a clear vision for DevOps adoption and define a strategic roadmap that aligns with the organization's goals.

- **Leading by Example:** Leaders should embody DevOps principles, promoting collaboration, continuous learning, and a culture of experimentation.

- **Empowering Teams:** Empowered teams are more likely to take ownership of their work, innovate, and drive improvements.

2. Building a DevOps Culture

Leaders should foster a culture that supports DevOps principles:

- **Open Communication:** Encourage transparent and open communication among teams, departments, and stakeholders.

- **Trust and Collaboration:** Build trust between development and operations teams, facilitating cross-functional collaboration.

- **Continuous Improvement:** Promote a culture of continuous improvement by rewarding innovation and learning from failures.

3. Leading DevOps Teams

DevOps leaders should lead by example and provide guidance to their teams:

- **Cross-Functional Teams:** Encourage the formation of cross-functional teams comprising developers, operations, and other relevant stakeholders.

- **Removing Obstacles:** Identify and remove obstacles that hinder team productivity and innovation.

- **Continuous Feedback:** Provide constructive feedback and support for individual and team growth.

4. Change Management

Change management is critical for ensuring a smooth transition to DevOps practices:

- **Assessment and Planning:** Begin by assessing the organization's current state and defining a DevOps adoption plan.

- **Stakeholder Engagement:** Involve stakeholders from various departments to gather input and ensure their concerns are addressed.

- **Pilot Projects:** Start with pilot projects to demonstrate the benefits of DevOps and gain early buy-in.

- **Training and Education:** Invest in training and education programs to upskill team members and ensure they are well-prepared for the changes.

- **Communication:** Maintain clear and regular communication about the progress of DevOps initiatives, addressing questions and concerns proactively.

5. Overcoming Resistance

Resistance to change is common in any organization. DevOps leaders can address resistance by:

- **Understanding Concerns:** Listen to and understand the concerns of team members and stakeholders.

- **Highlighting Benefits:** Communicate the benefits of DevOps, such as faster releases, improved quality, and enhanced collaboration.

- **Celebrating Success:** Celebrate achievements and successes resulting from DevOps practices to motivate teams.

- **Continuous Feedback:** Encourage feedback and use it to refine processes and address concerns.

6. Measuring Success

Leaders must define and track key performance indicators (KPIs) to measure the success of DevOps adoption:

- **Deployment Frequency:** How often code changes are deployed to production.

- **Lead Time:** The time it takes to move from code commit to deployment.

- **Change Failure Rate:** The percentage of deployments that result in failures.

- **Mean Time to Recovery (MTTR):** The time it takes to recover from incidents.

These metrics provide insights into the effectiveness of DevOps practices and help leaders make data-driven decisions.

7. Conclusion

Leadership and change management are integral components of DevOps adoption. Effective leadership sets the tone for a DevOps culture, guides teams, and drives the organization toward success. By embracing these principles, organizations can navigate the challenges of change, foster collaboration, and achieve the agility and efficiency that DevOps promises.

13.5. Future Trends and Evolutions in DevOps

DevOps is a dynamic field that continues to evolve to meet the changing needs of organizations and the demands of modern software development. In this section, we will explore some of the emerging trends and future directions in DevOps.

1. GitOps and Infrastructure as Code (IaC)

GitOps is gaining traction as a best practice for managing infrastructure and application deployments. It extends the principles of version control and collaboration from software development to infrastructure and operations. Git repositories become the source of truth for both application code and infrastructure configurations. This approach promotes transparency, repeatability, and automated deployments.

Infrastructure as Code (IaC) continues to be a fundamental part of DevOps. Tools like Terraform and AWS CloudFormation enable teams to define and provision infrastructure using code. The integration of IaC with CI/CD pipelines ensures that infrastructure changes are tested, versioned, and deployed with the same rigor as application code.

2. Kubernetes and Containers

Kubernetes has become the de facto standard for container orchestration. It simplifies the management of containerized applications, offering scalability, resilience, and portability. DevOps teams are increasingly adopting Kubernetes to streamline deployment and management.

Containers, particularly Docker containers, have become the building blocks of modern applications. They enable consistent environments from development through production, making it easier to achieve the "it works on my machine" problem. Containers are well-suited for microservices architectures, allowing teams to deploy, scale, and manage services independently.

3. Serverless Computing

Serverless computing, exemplified by platforms like AWS Lambda and Azure Functions, abstracts away server management, allowing developers to focus solely on code. Serverless is gaining popularity for event-driven and small-scale workloads, as it offers auto-scaling and cost optimization benefits. Integrating serverless components into DevOps pipelines requires new approaches to testing and monitoring.

4. Observability and Monitoring

As systems become more complex, observability becomes critical. Traditional monitoring tools are giving way to observability platforms that provide deep insights into application behavior, even in distributed and ephemeral environments. Techniques like distributed tracing, log aggregation, and metrics collection are essential for diagnosing issues and optimizing performance.

5. AIOps and Automation

Artificial Intelligence for IT Operations (AIOps) combines machine learning and big data analytics to automate and enhance various aspects of IT operations. AIOps can help predict and prevent incidents, automate routine tasks, and provide intelligent insights into system behavior.

6. Security as Code

DevSecOps is becoming a standard practice, with security integrated throughout the software development lifecycle. Security as Code involves the automation of security processes and the use of security tools as code dependencies. It ensures that security checks are performed continuously, and vulnerabilities are addressed promptly.

7. Edge Computing

Edge computing brings computation closer to data sources, reducing latency and enabling real-time processing. DevOps teams must adapt to managing and deploying applications at the edge, which presents new challenges in terms of infrastructure, networking, and security.

8. Hybrid and Multi-Cloud Deployments

Many organizations are adopting hybrid cloud and multi-cloud strategies to balance cost, performance, and compliance requirements. DevOps practices must accommodate the complexities of managing applications across diverse cloud environments.

9. Cultural Evolution

DevOps is not just about tools and processes; it's a cultural shift. Organizations will continue to focus on fostering a culture of collaboration, experimentation, and continuous learning. Leadership plays a critical role in driving cultural change.

In conclusion, DevOps is a continuously evolving field driven by technology advancements and the changing landscape of software development. Staying informed about these emerging trends and adopting relevant practices can help organizations remain competitive, agile, and efficient in delivering high-quality software to meet customer needs.

Chapter 14: Scaling Azure DevOps for Large Enterprises

14.1. Challenges in Scaling DevOps Practices

Scaling DevOps practices in large enterprises presents a unique set of challenges and opportunities. While DevOps principles have proven effective in improving software delivery in organizations of all sizes, the complexities of large enterprises introduce additional considerations. In this section, we will explore the challenges that large enterprises face when scaling DevOps and strategies to overcome them.

1. Silos and Organizational Structure

Large enterprises often have well-established silos and hierarchies that can hinder the collaboration and communication essential for DevOps. Different teams may have their own tools, processes, and objectives. Breaking down these silos and fostering cross-functional teams is crucial for successful DevOps adoption.

2. Legacy Systems and Technical Debt

Legacy systems and technical debt are common in large enterprises. These systems may lack automation, testing, and version control, making them challenging to integrate into modern DevOps pipelines. Strategies for gradually modernizing legacy systems while maintaining business continuity are essential.

3. Compliance and Regulatory Requirements

Large enterprises frequently operate in highly regulated industries, such as finance and healthcare, which have strict compliance and security requirements. DevOps practices must align with these regulations, and compliance-as-code approaches should be implemented to automate and audit compliance checks.

4. Scale and Complexity

Large enterprises manage extensive infrastructure, applications, and teams across various geographical locations. Scaling DevOps to accommodate this complexity requires robust automation, monitoring, and orchestration solutions. The use of Infrastructure as Code (IaC) and containerization can help manage scale.

5. Culture and Change Management

Cultural change is a significant challenge when scaling DevOps. Large enterprises may have deeply ingrained traditional practices and resistance to change. Leadership must drive cultural transformation by promoting DevOps values, continuous learning, and experimentation.

6. Toolchain Integration

Large enterprises often use a variety of tools and technologies across different teams and departments. Ensuring seamless integration between these tools, creating standardized pipelines, and adopting DevOps toolchains that support the organization's diverse needs are critical.

7. Performance and Scalability Testing

With large user bases and critical applications, performance and scalability testing are paramount. DevOps practices should incorporate automated performance testing to identify bottlenecks and optimize applications for peak performance.

8. Monitoring and Observability

Monitoring at scale requires robust solutions to track application and infrastructure health. Implementing observability practices with distributed tracing, log aggregation, and real-time analytics is essential for detecting and resolving issues quickly.

9. Talent and Skills Gap

Hiring and retaining skilled DevOps professionals can be a challenge in a competitive job market. Large enterprises should invest in training and upskilling their workforce to bridge the skills gap and build a strong DevOps team.

10. Cost Management

Large enterprises must optimize cloud costs as they scale DevOps practices. Implementing cost management and governance strategies, such as resource tagging, budgeting, and automated cost alerts, helps control expenditure.

In summary, scaling DevOps in large enterprises requires a strategic approach that addresses organizational, technical, and cultural challenges. By breaking down silos, modernizing legacy systems, ensuring compliance, and investing in culture and skills, large enterprises can harness the power of DevOps to deliver software faster, with higher quality, and at scale. In the following sections of this chapter, we will delve into specific strategies and best practices for successfully scaling Azure DevOps in large enterprises.

14.2. Azure DevOps at Enterprise Scale

When scaling Azure DevOps for large enterprises, it's crucial to understand how to leverage the platform effectively to meet the unique demands of a large organization. Azure DevOps offers a set of features and best practices tailored to address the challenges faced by enterprises. In this section, we will explore how to utilize Azure DevOps at an enterprise scale.

1. Project Hierarchy and Organization

Large enterprises often have a multitude of projects, each with its teams and repositories. Azure DevOps provides a hierarchical structure to manage these projects efficiently. Create a logical organization with multiple projects and establish a clear hierarchy for teams and repositories within each project.

- Enterprise Organization

- Business Unit 1

- Project 1

- Team A

- Team B

- Project 2

- Team C

- Business Unit 2

- Project 3

- Team D

2. Permissions and Access Control

Implement robust access control to ensure that only authorized personnel can access and modify resources. Azure DevOps allows for fine-grained permissions at the organization, project, and repository levels. Define roles and permissions that align with your organization's security policies.

3. Customization and Templates

Customize Azure DevOps to fit your enterprise's specific needs. Create templates for work items, pipelines, and repositories to standardize processes across projects. Define branching strategies and naming conventions that streamline development workflows.

4. Scalable Build and Release Pipelines

As the number of applications and services grows, build and release pipelines must be scalable. Use YAML-based pipelines to define build and deployment configurations as code. Leverage agent pools and deployment groups to distribute workloads efficiently.

5. Reporting and Analytics

Monitor and analyze project and portfolio performance using Azure DevOps' reporting and analytics capabilities. Create dashboards and reports to gain insights into work progress, test results, and code quality. Make data-driven decisions to optimize processes.

6. Integration with Third-Party Tools

Large enterprises often rely on a variety of tools for different purposes. Azure DevOps provides extensive integration options with third-party tools and services. Integrate with your existing tools, such as JIRA, Slack, or ServiceNow, to streamline workflows and communication.

7. Pipeline Automation

Implement automation throughout the software delivery lifecycle. Automate code builds, tests, and deployments to ensure consistency and reduce manual errors. Use release gates and approval workflows to maintain control over the deployment process.

8. Monitoring and Alerting

Set up comprehensive monitoring and alerting for applications and infrastructure. Azure DevOps integrates with Azure Monitor and Application Insights for real-time performance monitoring. Configure alerts to proactively detect and address issues.

9. Security and Compliance

Prioritize security and compliance in your DevOps processes. Implement security scanning and vulnerability assessments in your pipelines. Leverage Azure Key Vault for secure secrets and key management. Conduct regular security audits and compliance checks.

10. Cost Management

Large enterprises often operate at scale in the cloud. Implement cost management practices to control cloud expenditure. Use Azure Cost Management and Budgets to set spending limits and monitor resource costs.

11. Disaster Recovery and High Availability

Plan for disaster recovery and high availability of your DevOps infrastructure. Replicate critical resources across multiple regions and implement backup and restore procedures. Ensure that your DevOps platform can recover from failures swiftly.

In conclusion, Azure DevOps offers a comprehensive set of features and best practices to support enterprise-scale software development and delivery. By organizing projects, managing access, customizing processes, and automating workflows, large enterprises can harness the full potential of Azure DevOps to drive collaboration, efficiency, and innovation across their organization. The following sections of this chapter will delve deeper into specific strategies and case studies showcasing successful implementations of Azure DevOps at enterprise scale.

14.3. Managing Large and Complex Projects

Managing large and complex projects in Azure DevOps presents unique challenges and opportunities. In this section, we will explore strategies and best practices for effectively handling such projects.

1. Project Structure and Organization

In a large and complex project, maintaining a clear project structure is essential. Consider dividing the project into logical components or modules, each with its repositories, pipelines, and teams. A hierarchical structure helps streamline project management and allows teams to focus on specific areas.

- Large Project

- Module A

- Repository A1

- Team A1

- Module B

- Repository B1

- Team B1

- Module C

- Repository C1

- Team C1

2. Work Item Tracking and Backlogs

Use Azure Boards to manage work items efficiently. Create backlogs and boards specific to each module or component within the project. Prioritize work items, assign them to teams, and establish clear dependencies between tasks.

3. Branching and Version Control

Implement branching strategies tailored to your project's needs. Large projects may require feature branches, release branches, and hotfix branches. Ensure that branching and merging processes are well-defined and understood by the development teams.

4. Pipeline Orchestration

In complex projects, multiple pipelines may be required to build and deploy different components. Use pipeline orchestration to coordinate the execution of pipelines across modules. Implement trigger mechanisms to automate pipeline execution when changes occur.

5. Cross-Team Collaboration

Large projects often involve multiple teams working on different aspects of the software. Encourage cross-team collaboration through regular meetings, joint sprint planning, and shared communication channels. Ensure that dependencies between teams are well-documented and managed.

6. Testing and Quality Assurance

Implement a robust testing strategy that covers all modules and components. Use Azure Test Plans to design test cases and automated tests. Integrate testing into the CI/CD pipeline to ensure that code changes are thoroughly tested before deployment.

7. Reporting and Monitoring

Leverage Azure DevOps' reporting and monitoring capabilities to gain insights into project progress and quality. Create dashboards and reports that provide visibility into work item status, build success rates, and test results. Set up alerts for critical events.

8. Documentation and Knowledge Sharing

Maintain comprehensive documentation for the project, including architecture diagrams, design documents, and coding guidelines. Foster a culture of knowledge sharing among team members. Use wikis and documentation tools within Azure DevOps to centralize information.

9. Security and Compliance

Large projects often handle sensitive data and have strict security requirements. Implement security scanning and threat mitigation in your pipelines. Ensure compliance with industry standards and regulations, and conduct regular security audits.

10. Scaling Resources

As the project scales, be prepared to allocate additional resources, both in terms of infrastructure and personnel. Utilize Azure DevOps' scalability features, such as agent pools and parallel jobs, to accommodate increased workload.

11. Change Management

Implement a robust change management process to handle modifications to project scope, requirements, or design. Ensure that changes are properly documented, reviewed, and approved by stakeholders.

12. Continuous Improvement

Regularly assess the project's processes and performance. Identify bottlenecks, areas for improvement, and opportunities to optimize workflows. Encourage a culture of continuous improvement among team members.

In conclusion, managing large and complex projects in Azure DevOps requires careful planning, coordination, and the adoption of best practices. By organizing the project structure, implementing efficient workflows, and fostering collaboration among teams, organizations can successfully navigate the challenges posed by large-scale software development initiatives. This section has provided an overview of strategies to manage large projects, and the following sections will delve into case studies and real-world examples of successful implementations in complex project environments.

14.4. Security and Compliance at Scale

Security and compliance are paramount in large enterprises, especially when dealing with complex projects. In this section, we'll explore strategies for maintaining security and compliance at scale within Azure DevOps.

1. Access Control and Permissions

When dealing with large teams and complex projects, managing access control and permissions becomes critical. Azure DevOps provides robust access control mechanisms. Implement role-based access control (RBAC) to assign appropriate permissions to individuals or groups based on their roles and responsibilities. Regularly review and audit permissions to ensure that only authorized personnel have access to sensitive resources.

Example RBAC Roles:

- Contributor: Can create and manage resources within a project.

- Reader: Has read-only access to project resources.

- Project Administrator: Manages project settings and permissions.

- Security Administrator: Focuses on security-related tasks and configurations.

2. Compliance Policies and Standards

Define compliance policies and standards specific to your organization's industry and regulatory requirements. Azure DevOps allows you to enforce policies using Azure Policy, Azure Blueprints, and custom policies. Ensure that these policies cover aspects such as data security, encryption, access controls, and auditing.

3. Continuous Compliance Monitoring

Implement continuous compliance monitoring to track adherence to policies and standards. Azure Policy and Azure Security Center can help automate compliance assessments. Set up alerts and notifications for policy violations, and take proactive measures to remediate non-compliance issues.

4. Secure DevOps Practices

Incorporate secure DevOps practices into your development pipelines. Implement security scans and vulnerability assessments in your CI/CD process. Use tools like Azure DevOps Security Center and Azure Security Center to identify and remediate security issues in your infrastructure and applications.

Example CI/CD Security Checks:

- Static Application Security Testing (SAST)

- Dynamic Application Security Testing (DAST)

- Dependency Scanning

- Container Scanning

- Credential Scanning

5. Secrets Management

Effectively manage secrets, keys, and certificates used in your applications and infrastructure. Azure Key Vault is a secure and scalable solution for secrets management. Integrate Key Vault with your pipelines to securely store and retrieve secrets during deployment.

Example Key Vault Usage in Pipelines:

- Storing database connection strings

- Managing API keys and tokens

- Securing SSL/TLS certificates

6. Data Protection and Encryption

Implement data protection and encryption mechanisms to safeguard sensitive information. Use Azure services like Azure SQL Database with Transparent Data Encryption (TDE) or Azure Disk Encryption to encrypt data at rest. Employ encryption in transit using protocols like HTTPS and TLS.

7. Identity and Access Management (IAM)

Leverage Azure Active Directory (Azure AD) for robust identity and access management. Implement single sign-on (SSO) and multi-factor authentication (MFA) for enhanced security. Ensure that users have the appropriate level of access based on their roles and responsibilities.

8. Auditing and Logging

Enable auditing and logging for Azure DevOps and related Azure services. Azure Monitor and Azure Security Center provide centralized logging and auditing capabilities. Maintain logs for security incident investigations, compliance reporting, and forensic analysis.

9. Incident Response and Recovery

Establish an incident response plan to address security breaches and incidents promptly. Define incident severity levels, response procedures, and communication protocols. Conduct regular tabletop exercises to ensure that your team is prepared to handle security incidents.

10. Third-Party Security Solutions

Consider third-party security solutions that integrate with Azure DevOps for advanced threat detection, vulnerability scanning, and compliance reporting. Evaluate and select tools that align with your organization's security requirements.

11. Security Training and Awareness

Invest in security training and awareness programs for your development and operations teams. Security awareness sessions help educate team members about security best practices and potential threats.

12. Documentation and Compliance Reports

Maintain detailed documentation of your security controls and compliance measures. Generate compliance reports and documentation required for audits and regulatory assessments.

In summary, ensuring security and compliance at scale in large enterprises requires a combination of access control, policies, continuous monitoring, secure DevOps practices, and robust incident response procedures. By implementing these strategies, organizations can mitigate security risks and maintain regulatory compliance while managing complex projects within Azure DevOps.

14.5. Case Studies: Enterprise Success with Azure DevOps

In this section, we'll delve into real-world case studies of large enterprises that have successfully adopted Azure DevOps at scale. These examples illustrate how organizations have leveraged Azure DevOps to improve productivity, streamline processes, and achieve their business goals.

1. Microsoft

As the creator of Azure DevOps, Microsoft's own experience with the platform is noteworthy. Microsoft utilizes Azure DevOps for the development of its extensive portfolio of software products, including Windows, Office, and Azure itself. The company has transformed its development processes, achieving faster release cycles, better collaboration, and increased efficiency. Microsoft's adoption of Azure DevOps serves as a testament to the platform's scalability and capabilities.

2. Siemens

Siemens, a global leader in technology and industrial solutions, implemented Azure DevOps to enhance its software development practices. By adopting a DevOps approach, Siemens reduced development cycle times by up to 40%. Azure DevOps enabled them to automate repetitive tasks, improve testing, and achieve higher code quality. The result was faster innovation and more reliable products for their customers.

3. GE Healthcare

GE Healthcare, a subsidiary of General Electric, leveraged Azure DevOps to optimize its healthcare software development processes.

The company needed to comply with strict regulatory requirements for its medical devices. Azure DevOps provided the necessary tools for traceability, compliance reporting, and automated testing. GE Healthcare achieved improved quality control, reduced time-to-market, and ensured adherence to regulatory standards.

4. Adobe

Adobe, a leading provider of creative software and digital marketing solutions, adopted Azure DevOps to streamline its application development lifecycle. By integrating Azure DevOps with Adobe's existing tools and systems, the company achieved faster delivery of new features and bug fixes to its customers. The automation capabilities of Azure DevOps allowed Adobe to scale its development efforts efficiently.

5. Accenture

Accenture, a global consulting and professional services firm, integrated Azure DevOps into its client projects to accelerate software delivery. By implementing best practices and Azure DevOps tools, Accenture reduced manual intervention in the deployment process. This led to significant time savings and higher predictability in project deliveries. Clients benefited from more agile and cost-effective solutions.

6. Boeing

Boeing, a renowned aerospace and defense company, employed Azure DevOps to manage its complex projects, including aircraft design and manufacturing. Azure DevOps helped Boeing enhance collaboration among geographically dispersed teams, ensure version control for critical documents, and maintain strict quality and compliance standards in the aerospace industry.

7. Fujitsu

Fujitsu, a global information technology company, embraced Azure DevOps to optimize its software development and delivery processes. By adopting a DevOps culture and leveraging Azure DevOps tools, Fujitsu reduced manual intervention, improved code quality, and accelerated time-to-market for its solutions. The company's success with Azure DevOps exemplifies its applicability across diverse industries.

8. Schlumberger

Schlumberger, an oilfield services company, utilized Azure DevOps to enhance its software development practices for the energy sector. Azure DevOps enabled Schlumberger to improve collaboration between development and operations teams, resulting in more stable and reliable software solutions for the energy industry.

These case studies underscore the versatility of Azure DevOps in meeting the needs of large enterprises across various domains. Whether in technology, healthcare, aviation, or consulting, organizations have achieved remarkable improvements in efficiency, quality, and innovation by embracing Azure DevOps at scale. These success stories serve as inspiration for enterprises considering the adoption of DevOps practices and Azure DevOps as a foundational platform.

15.1. Planning and Strategy for Migration

Migrating to Azure DevOps from other development and project management platforms is a significant undertaking that requires careful planning and a well-defined strategy. Whether you are moving from legacy systems, other cloud-based solutions, or on-premises tools, a successful migration can greatly enhance your team's productivity and collaboration. In this section, we will explore the key considerations and steps involved in planning and executing a migration to Azure DevOps.

1. Assessment and Inventory

Before embarking on a migration, it's crucial to assess your existing tools, processes, and workflows. Identify the software development, project management, and collaboration tools currently in use. Document the data and artifacts stored in these systems, including source code repositories, work items, project plans, and documentation.

Create an inventory of the following:

- Source code repositories and version control systems.
- Work items, user stories, bugs, and backlog items.
- Test cases and test plans.
- Build and release pipelines.
- Documentation and artifacts related to projects.
- Access control and permissions.

2. Define Migration Goals and Scope

Clearly define the goals and scope of your migration project. Determine what you want to achieve with Azure DevOps and how it aligns with your organization's objectives. Consider factors such as improved collaboration, faster software delivery, enhanced reporting and analytics, and compliance requirements.

Set realistic expectations and prioritize the order in which you will migrate different components. For example, you might start with source code repositories and then move on to work items and build pipelines.

3. Select Migration Tools and Methods

Azure DevOps provides various tools and methods for migration, depending on the source systems and data you need to transfer. Evaluate the available options and choose the most suitable ones for your migration needs.

Some common migration methods and tools include:

- **Azure DevOps Data Import Service:** This service supports data migration from various source systems, including Jira, GitHub, and TFS. It simplifies the migration of work items, comments, and attachments.

- **Git Import Tool:** If you are migrating source code repositories, the Git Import tool can help you import Git repositories from other hosting services like GitHub or Bitbucket.

- **Manual Migration:** In some cases, manual migration might be the best approach, especially for complex data structures or legacy systems. This involves exporting data from the source system and then importing it into Azure DevOps manually.

4. Data Mapping and Transformation

Ensure that you have a clear understanding of the mapping and transformation requirements between the source data and Azure

DevOps data structures. Work on mapping the source fields to their corresponding fields in Azure DevOps. If needed, perform data transformations to ensure that the data retains its integrity and relevance after migration.

5. Test the Migration Process

Before executing a full-scale migration, perform testing with a subset of your data to identify and address any issues or inconsistencies. Test the migration of source code, work items, test cases, and other artifacts to verify that the data appears correctly in Azure DevOps.

6. User Training and Change Management

Prepare your team for the migration by providing training and resources. Communicate the upcoming changes and ensure that team members are familiar with Azure DevOps and its features. Implement a change management plan to address any resistance or challenges that may arise during the migration process.

7. Execute the Migration

Once you are confident in your migration plan and have addressed any issues from testing, execute the migration according to your defined scope and sequence. Monitor the migration process closely and be prepared to address any unexpected issues that may arise.

8. Post-Migration Validation

After the migration is complete, validate that all data has been successfully transferred to Azure DevOps. Conduct a thorough review of source code, work items, test cases, and other artifacts to ensure accuracy and completeness.

9. Optimization and Continuous Improvement

Once your team is fully operational in Azure DevOps, continue to optimize your processes and workflows. Take advantage of Azure DevOps' reporting and analytics capabilities to gain insights into your development projects and identify areas for improvement.

10. Documentation and Best Practices

Document the migration process, including any challenges faced and solutions implemented. Share best practices and lessons learned with your team to facilitate future migrations and ensure ongoing success with Azure DevOps.

In summary, migrating to Azure DevOps requires careful planning, assessment, and execution. By following a structured approach and considering the key factors mentioned above, you can ensure a successful transition to Azure DevOps and harness its full potential for your organization's software development and project management needs.

15.2. Migrating Source Code and Repositories

Migrating source code and repositories is a critical aspect of transitioning to Azure DevOps. In this section, we will delve into the specifics of migrating your source code from existing version control systems to Azure DevOps, whether you are using Git, SVN, Mercurial, or another VCS. A well-executed source code migration ensures that your development teams can continue their work seamlessly in Azure DevOps.

1. Selecting the Right Migration Approach

Before you begin the migration process, it's essential to choose the appropriate migration approach based on your current version control system (VCS) and the goals of your migration. Here are some common migration scenarios:

- **Migrating from Git:** If you are currently using Git, migrating to Azure DevOps is relatively straightforward. You can use the Git Import Tool provided by Azure DevOps, which allows you to import Git repositories from other hosting services like GitHub, Bitbucket, or GitLab.

- **Migrating from Subversion (SVN):** Migrating from SVN to Azure DevOps typically involves using a tool like svn2git to convert your SVN repositories into Git repositories. Once you have Git repositories, you can use the Git Import Tool or push them directly to Azure DevOps.

- **Migrating from Mercurial:** Similar to SVN, if you are using Mercurial, you can convert your Mercurial repositories to Git using tools like hg-git or fast-export. Once in Git format, you can proceed with the migration.

- **Migrating from Other VCS:** For other version control systems, the process may vary. It often involves exporting the repository's history and data in a format that can be imported into Azure DevOps.

2. Preparing for the Migration

Regardless of the source VCS, there are several preparation steps to consider:

- **Backup:** Before starting the migration, ensure that you have a backup of your existing repositories and their complete history. This is a precautionary measure in case anything goes wrong during the migration process.

- **Access and Permissions:** Make sure that you have the necessary permissions and access rights for both the source VCS and Azure DevOps. You'll need appropriate permissions to read and write to both systems.

- **Mapping and Configuration:** Understand how your existing VCS maps to Git repositories. Plan how you want to structure your repositories in Azure DevOps, including branch naming conventions and permissions.

3. Performing the Migration

The migration process can vary based on the approach you selected:

- **Using the Git Import Tool:** If you are migrating Git repositories, you can use Azure DevOps' built-in Git Import Tool. This tool simplifies the process by providing a step-by-step wizard for migrating repositories from other Git hosting services.

- **Converting and Pushing Git Repositories:** For SVN, Mercurial, or other VCS, you'll need to convert the repositories to Git format and then push them to Azure

DevOps. This often involves using command-line tools like git-svn for SVN or hg-git for Mercurial.

4. Verification and Testing

After migration, it's crucial to verify that the repositories in Azure DevOps match the source repositories. You should validate:

- **Commit History:** Check that the commit history has been migrated accurately, including all commits, branches, and tags.

- **Branches and Tags:** Ensure that branches and tags are correctly mapped and named in Azure DevOps.

- **Permissions:** Verify that access permissions and branch-level permissions are correctly set up.

- **Integration:** If your repositories are integrated with other systems (e.g., CI/CD pipelines), confirm that these integrations are working as expected in Azure DevOps.

5. Communication and Training

Inform your development teams about the successful migration and any changes to the repository structure or workflow. Provide training on Azure DevOps' Git-based version control system, including branching strategies and best practices.

6. Backup and Rollback Plan

Despite careful planning, issues can arise during migration. Always have a rollback plan and a backup of your source code and repositories in case you need to revert to your previous VCS temporarily.

7. Continuous Integration and Deployment (CI/CD) Integration

Integrate your migrated repositories with your CI/CD pipelines in Azure DevOps. Ensure that build and release processes work seamlessly with the new Git repositories.

Migrating source code and repositories is a significant step in adopting Azure DevOps, and it requires careful planning and execution. By following these best practices and considering your specific VCS and migration goals, you can ensure a smooth transition for your development teams, allowing them to take full advantage of Azure DevOps' capabilities for version control and collaboration.

15.3. Migrating Build and Release Pipelines

Migrating build and release pipelines is a crucial part of transitioning to Azure DevOps. In this section, we will explore the steps and best practices involved in migrating your existing build and release processes to Azure DevOps pipelines. These pipelines are responsible for automating the build, testing, and deployment of your applications and services.

1. Assessing Current Pipelines

Before migrating your build and release pipelines, it's essential to assess your current setup. Document your existing build and release processes, including the tools, scripts, and configurations used. Identify the following:

- **Build Definitions:** List all the build definitions used for compiling and packaging your applications.

• **Release Definitions:** Document the release definitions that automate deployments to different environments.

• **Dependencies:** Note any dependencies on external systems, libraries, or services in your existing pipelines.

2. Azure DevOps Pipelines

Azure DevOps provides robust build and release pipeline capabilities. You will typically use two types of pipelines:

• **Build Pipelines:** These define how your source code is built, compiled, and packaged into artifacts. You can use YAML or classic editor-based configurations for build pipelines.

• **Release Pipelines:** These automate the deployment of your applications to various environments (e.g., development, staging, production). Release pipelines are typically defined using YAML-based configurations.

3. Creating Azure DevOps Pipelines

Here's a high-level process for creating Azure DevOps pipelines:

a. Build Pipelines

1. **Configure Build Agents:** Ensure you have the necessary build agents installed and configured in your Azure DevOps organization to match your requirements.
2. **Create a New Build Pipeline:** In Azure DevOps, navigate to the Pipelines section and create a new build pipeline. You can choose between YAML or the classic editor for defining your pipeline.

3. **Define Build Steps:** Specify the steps required to build your code, run tests, and generate artifacts. This includes specifying the source code repository, triggers, and build agents.
4. **Artifact Publishing:** Publish build artifacts (e.g., binaries, libraries) so they can be used in release pipelines.
5. **Integration:** If you have external integrations (e.g., code scanning tools, code quality checks), configure them as part of your build pipeline.

b. Release Pipelines

1. **Create a New Release Pipeline:** In Azure DevOps, go to the Pipelines section and create a new release pipeline. Use YAML-based configuration to define your release stages and tasks.
2. **Define Deployment Stages:** Define deployment stages for each environment (e.g., development, QA, production). Specify deployment triggers, approvals, and conditions.
3. **Artifact Integration:** Link your release pipeline to the build artifacts generated by your build pipeline. Define which artifacts should be deployed to each environment.
4. **Configuration Management:** Manage configuration settings for each environment within the release pipeline, ensuring that your application behaves correctly in each stage.

4. Migration Process

Migrating your build and release pipelines involves recreating your existing pipeline configurations in Azure DevOps. Here's a step-by-step migration process:

a. Build Pipelines

1. **YAML Conversion:** If your existing build pipeline uses YAML configurations, transitioning to Azure DevOps YAML pipelines is straightforward. Copy and adapt your existing YAML definitions to Azure DevOps YAML.
2. **Classic Editor Migration:** If you are using the classic editor, manually recreate your build pipeline in Azure DevOps by configuring the build steps, triggers, and agents.

b. Release Pipelines

1. **YAML Definition:** Define your release pipeline using YAML. Specify stages, tasks, and deployment conditions as code.
2. **Manual Recreate:** If your existing release pipelines are not defined in YAML, manually recreate them in Azure DevOps using the YAML-based release pipeline configuration.

5. Testing and Validation

After migrating your pipelines, thoroughly test them to ensure they function as expected. Verify that builds complete successfully, and deployments to various environments proceed without issues. Address any discrepancies or errors that arise during testing.

6. Rollback Plan

Have a rollback plan in place in case the migration leads to unexpected problems or issues. This plan should include steps to revert to your previous build and release processes if needed.

7. Documentation and Training

Document the new Azure DevOps build and release pipeline configurations and provide training to your team members involved in managing and using these pipelines.

8. Incremental Migration

Consider an incremental migration approach where you migrate one project or application at a time. This reduces the complexity and risk associated with a large-scale migration.

Migrating build and release pipelines is a critical step in adopting Azure DevOps, as it enables you to automate and streamline your software delivery processes. Careful planning, testing, and validation are essential to ensure a successful transition and minimal disruption to your development and deployment workflows.

15.4. Data Migration and Integration Challenges

When migrating to Azure DevOps from other platforms, one significant challenge that organizations often face is handling data migration and integration. Data migration involves moving various types of data, including source code repositories, work items, build configurations, release definitions, and more, from the existing system to Azure DevOps. This process is crucial to ensure that historical data and ongoing work are seamlessly transitioned. However, it comes with its own set of complexities and considerations.

1. Data Mapping and Transformation

One of the initial challenges is mapping data from the source system to Azure DevOps. The data structures and fields in the existing system may differ from those in Azure DevOps. Organizations need to define mapping rules and potentially perform data transformations to ensure data consistency and integrity during migration.

2. Data Cleanup and Quality

Before migrating, it's essential to clean up and validate data. This includes identifying and resolving duplicate records, ensuring data accuracy, and verifying that all dependencies and relationships are correctly represented in Azure DevOps.

3. Data Volume and Performance

Handling large volumes of data can impact migration performance. Organizations must assess the volume of data to be migrated and plan accordingly. This may involve optimizing data migration scripts, using bulk import/export methods, or leveraging Azure services like Azure Data Factory for efficient data movement.

4. Data Security and Compliance

Maintaining data security and compliance during migration is crucial, especially when dealing with sensitive or regulated data. Ensure that data encryption, access controls, and auditing mechanisms are in place both in the source system and Azure DevOps.

5. Integration with Legacy Systems

In many cases, organizations have existing systems and tools that need to integrate with Azure DevOps. This may include integrating with legacy version control systems, project management tools, or test management tools. Ensuring smooth integration is vital to avoid disruptions in workflows.

6. Custom Data Types and Workflows

Organizations often have custom data types, fields, and workflows in their existing systems. Replicating these customizations in Azure DevOps may require additional planning and development effort. Azure DevOps provides customization capabilities, but aligning them with existing processes can be intricate.

7. Historical Data Preservation

Preserving historical data is essential for tracking progress, compliance, and reporting purposes. Organizations must determine how far back they need to migrate historical data and ensure that all relevant historical records are included in the migration.

8. Testing and Validation

Data migration should undergo rigorous testing and validation to ensure data consistency and correctness. This includes verifying that work items, links, attachments, and historical data are accurately migrated.

9. User Training and Adoption

Once data migration is complete, users need to adapt to the new system. Providing adequate training and support is crucial to ensure that team members can effectively use Azure DevOps for their work.

10. Rollback Planning

Despite careful planning, issues may arise during data migration. Having a rollback plan in place is essential to revert to the previous state if needed without data loss or disruption.

Addressing these challenges requires careful planning, documentation, and collaboration among teams responsible for data migration and integration. It's essential to engage stakeholders from both the technical and business sides to ensure a successful transition to Azure DevOps while preserving data integrity and minimizing disruptions.

15.5. Post-Migration Best Practices and Optimization

After successfully migrating to Azure DevOps from another platform, organizations must focus on post-migration best practices and optimization to ensure long-term success and maximize the benefits of the new environment. Here are key considerations and strategies for this phase:

1. Data Validation and Reconciliation

Start by thoroughly validating and reconciling the migrated data. Ensure that all work items, source code repositories, build pipelines, and other artifacts are in the expected state. This validation is critical to spot any data inconsistencies or issues that might have arisen during the migration process.

2. Configuration Review

Review and fine-tune the configuration settings in Azure DevOps. This includes revisiting project configurations, permissions, security settings, and notification rules. Ensure that the configuration aligns with your team's workflows and requirements.

3. Customization and Automation

Leverage Azure DevOps' customization and automation capabilities to streamline your workflows further. Implement custom work item types, fields, and process templates to match your team's specific needs. Create automation scripts or use Azure DevOps services like Azure Logic Apps to automate repetitive tasks and notifications.

4. Integration and Tooling

Continue integrating Azure DevOps with other tools and systems used in your organization. Ensure that data flows seamlessly between Azure DevOps and external systems, such as project management tools, test management platforms, and version control systems. Monitor these integrations to identify and resolve any issues promptly.

5. Performance Optimization

Regularly monitor the performance of Azure DevOps to identify bottlenecks or slowdowns. Optimize your pipelines, builds, and releases for efficiency. Consider using caching mechanisms, parallelization, and agent pooling to improve build and deployment times. Azure DevOps provides performance monitoring and diagnostics tools to help with this.

6. Security and Compliance

Maintain a strong focus on security and compliance post-migration. Regularly review and update access controls, permissions, and security policies. Ensure that sensitive data is adequately protected and that compliance requirements are met. Regular security audits and assessments can help in this regard.

7. User Training and Adoption

Continuously invest in user training and adoption programs. Ensure that your team members are familiar with the full range of Azure DevOps features and best practices. Encourage the use of collaboration tools, code reviews, and automated testing to improve productivity.

8. Reporting and Analytics

Make the most of Azure DevOps' reporting and analytics capabilities. Create customized dashboards and reports to gain insights into project progress, code quality, and team performance. Regularly review these metrics to identify areas for improvement.

9. Scaling and Growth

As your organization grows or project complexity increases, assess whether your Azure DevOps setup can scale effectively. Consider adopting Azure DevOps at an enterprise scale, which offers additional capabilities for large organizations.

10. Feedback and Continuous Improvement

Lastly, establish a feedback loop for continuous improvement. Encourage team members to provide feedback on the Azure DevOps environment, including pain points and suggestions for enhancement. Use this feedback to iteratively refine your processes and configurations.

By following these post-migration best practices and optimization strategies, organizations can fully realize the benefits of Azure

DevOps, improve collaboration, accelerate software delivery, and adapt to evolving project requirements effectively. Regularly revisit and adjust your approach to align with changing needs and industry best practices.

Chapter 16: Implementing DevSecOps in Azure DevOps

Section 16.1: Introduction to DevSecOps

DevSecOps is a modern approach to software development that integrates security practices into the DevOps process. While traditional development and operations practices have often treated security as a separate concern, DevSecOps recognizes the need to address security at every stage of the software development lifecycle. This proactive approach aims to identify and remediate security vulnerabilities early in the development process, reducing the risk of security breaches and ensuring the delivery of more secure and compliant software.

The Evolution of DevSecOps

DevSecOps emerged as a response to the growing need for organizations to enhance their security posture in an increasingly digital and interconnected world. Traditional security practices, which typically involve manual security assessments performed late in the development cycle, have proven to be inadequate in addressing the rapidly evolving threat landscape.

In the past, security was often viewed as a hindrance to the rapid delivery of software. However, as high-profile security breaches became more common, organizations realized the importance of integrating security seamlessly into their development and deployment pipelines. This realization gave rise to DevSecOps, which aims to make security an integral part of DevOps culture and practices.

Key Concepts of DevSecOps

1. **Shift-Left Security**: DevSecOps encourages a "shift-left" approach to security, where security considerations are moved as early as possible in the development process. Developers are empowered to identify and fix security issues during the coding phase, reducing the cost and effort required to address them later in the pipeline.
2. **Automation**: Automation is a fundamental aspect of DevSecOps. Security scans, vulnerability assessments, and compliance checks are automated and integrated into the CI/CD pipeline. This ensures that security checks are consistent, repeatable, and don't introduce delays in the software delivery process.
3. **Continuous Monitoring**: DevSecOps promotes continuous monitoring of applications and infrastructure in production. Real-time monitoring and automated alerting help organizations detect and respond to security incidents promptly.
4. **Collaboration**: Collaboration between development, operations, and security teams is crucial in DevSecOps. Cross-functional teams work together to identify and mitigate security risks effectively. Communication and knowledge sharing are key components of this collaboration.

Benefits of DevSecOps

Implementing DevSecOps practices offers several benefits to organizations:

- **Improved Security**: By addressing security concerns early and continuously, DevSecOps reduces the likelihood of security breaches and vulnerabilities in production.

- **Faster Remediation**: Security issues are identified and remediated more quickly, reducing the time window for potential attacks.

- **Compliance**: DevSecOps helps organizations meet regulatory and compliance requirements by automating checks and documentation.

- **Cost Savings**: Fixing security issues earlier in the development process is less costly than addressing them in production.

- **Enhanced Reputation**: Building and delivering secure software enhances an organization's reputation and trustworthiness.

Challenges in DevSecOps

While DevSecOps offers significant advantages, it also presents challenges. Organizations may encounter resistance to change, skill gaps, and the need for cultural shifts to adopt DevSecOps successfully. Additionally, integrating security tools and practices into existing DevOps pipelines can be complex.

In this chapter, we will explore various aspects of implementing DevSecOps in Azure DevOps. From integrating security scans into your CI/CD pipelines to automating security practices, we will provide practical guidance to help you enhance the security of your software delivery process.

Section 16.2: Integrating Security into

DevOps Pipelines

Integrating security into DevOps pipelines is a fundamental aspect of implementing DevSecOps practices. By embedding security checks and processes directly into your CI/CD pipelines, you can identify and address security vulnerabilities early in the software development lifecycle. This section explores various strategies and best practices for integrating security seamlessly into your DevOps workflows.

Security as Code

One of the core principles of DevSecOps is treating security policies, checks, and configurations as code. This approach, known as "Security as Code," involves defining security controls and policies using code that can be versioned, tested, and automated.

For example, security policies can be codified using Infrastructure as Code (IaC) templates such as Azure Resource Manager (ARM) templates or Terraform scripts. These templates can include security configurations, such as network rules and access control settings, ensuring that security is consistently applied when provisioning resources.

Automated Security Scanning

Automated security scanning tools are essential components of DevSecOps pipelines. These tools automatically analyze your code, dependencies, and infrastructure for known security vulnerabilities, misconfigurations, and compliance violations. Common types of automated security scans include:

- **Static Application Security Testing (SAST)**: SAST tools analyze source code, bytecode, or binary code for security vulnerabilities. They identify issues like code injection, SQL injection, and insecure authentication methods.

- **Dynamic Application Security Testing (DAST)**: DAST tools test applications from the outside by simulating attacks. They help identify runtime vulnerabilities, such as insecure API endpoints and weak authentication mechanisms.

- **Container Security Scanning**: If you're using containerization, integrating container security scanning tools can help you detect vulnerabilities in container images and their dependencies.

- **Infrastructure as Code (IaC) Scanning**: For cloud deployments, IaC scanning tools can identify security issues in your infrastructure code, such as open ports or missing encryption settings.

Continuous Vulnerability Assessment

Continuous vulnerability assessment involves regularly scanning your application and infrastructure for new vulnerabilities and emerging threats. These assessments can be scheduled at predefined intervals or triggered by code changes. The goal is to ensure that your software remains secure as new vulnerabilities are discovered and patched.

Shift-Left Testing

Shift-Left Testing is a practice in which security testing is moved as early as possible in the development process. Developers are encouraged to perform security testing on their code before it's integrated into the main codebase. This approach not only reduces the cost of fixing security issues but also promotes a security-conscious development culture.

Security Gates

Security gates are automated checkpoints in your CI/CD pipeline where security checks are enforced. If a security check fails, the pipeline is halted until the issue is resolved. Security gates provide a strong mechanism for ensuring that security requirements are met before software is deployed.

Security Orchestration and Automation

Security orchestration and automation tools help streamline security incident response and remediation. They can automate the execution of predefined playbooks in response to security alerts or incidents. By automating repetitive security tasks, your security team can respond more effectively to threats and vulnerabilities.

In Azure DevOps, you can integrate security scanning tools, such as Azure Security Center or third-party solutions, directly into your pipelines. You can define security policies, automate scans, and enforce security gates to ensure that your applications meet security standards.

By adopting these practices and tools, you can effectively integrate security into your DevOps pipelines, reducing security risks and vulnerabilities in your software. In the following sections, we will delve deeper into specific security practices and demonstrate how to implement them in Azure DevOps.

Section 16.3: Security Automation and Tooling in Azure DevOps

Security automation and tooling play a crucial role in ensuring that your DevOps pipelines are secure and compliant with industry standards and best practices. Azure DevOps provides a range of built-in features and integrations with third-party security tools to help you automate security tasks and strengthen your security posture.

Azure DevOps Security Features

1. **Pipeline Security**: Azure DevOps offers security controls at the pipeline level. You can configure permissions to restrict who can create, edit, or trigger pipelines. Additionally, secrets and sensitive information, such as API keys and connection strings, can be securely stored in Azure Key Vault or Azure DevOps service connections.
2. **Role-Based Access Control (RBAC)**: Azure DevOps provides RBAC capabilities, allowing you to define granular permissions for users and teams. By assigning roles with the appropriate level of access, you can ensure that only authorized personnel can perform certain actions, such as creating or modifying pipelines.
3. **Security Scanning Integration**: Azure DevOps can integrate with various security scanning tools, both for code and infrastructure. For example, you can configure pipeline tasks to run static code analysis using tools like SonarQube or perform container security scans with tools like Trivy or Anchore.
4. **Pipeline Templates**: You can create reusable pipeline templates that include security checks and configurations. These templates can enforce security policies and best

practices across your organization's projects and pipelines.

5. **Policy Enforcement**: Azure DevOps allows you to define policies that enforce code quality and security standards. For instance, you can set policies that require code reviews, enforce branch protections, or check for security vulnerabilities in container images before deployment.

Azure DevOps Marketplace Integrations

The Azure DevOps Marketplace offers a wide range of security-related extensions and integrations. These extensions can enhance your security automation capabilities by adding specialized security checks, compliance reporting, and threat detection.

1. **Static Application Security Testing (SAST)**: You can integrate SAST tools like Checkmarx or Fortify into your pipelines using Marketplace extensions. These tools analyze your source code for vulnerabilities and provide detailed reports.
2. **Dynamic Application Security Testing (DAST)**: Marketplace extensions like OWASP ZAP or Netsparker enable you to perform DAST scans on your web applications during the pipeline execution. They help identify security issues such as SQL injection or cross-site scripting (XSS) vulnerabilities.
3. **Infrastructure as Code (IaC) Scanning**: To ensure the security of your cloud infrastructure deployments, you can use IaC scanning extensions like Checkov or Terrascan. These tools assess your Terraform or ARM templates for security compliance.
4. **Secrets Scanning**: Extensions like GitGuardian can automatically scan your repositories for exposed secrets, such as API keys or passwords, and notify you of potential

security risks.

5. **Security Compliance**: You can leverage extensions that provide compliance-as-code capabilities. These tools help you define, enforce, and assess security compliance standards in your pipelines.

Custom Security Checks

In addition to using existing security tools and integrations, you can develop custom security checks and automation scripts tailored to your organization's specific security requirements. Azure DevOps supports the execution of custom scripts within pipelines, allowing you to perform tasks like vulnerability scanning, compliance checks, or security testing using your preferred tools and languages.

By combining Azure DevOps' built-in security features, Marketplace extensions, and custom security automation, you can establish a robust security framework within your DevOps pipelines. This approach ensures that security is an integral part of your software development and delivery process, helping you identify and mitigate security risks early in the development lifecycle.

Section 16.4: Collaborative Security Practices

Collaboration is at the heart of DevSecOps, where security practices seamlessly integrate with development and operations processes. In this section, we'll explore collaborative security practices and how they enhance the security of your Azure DevOps pipelines.

Security Champions

One of the key elements of collaborative security is the concept of "Security Champions." Security Champions are individuals within your development and operations teams who have a strong understanding of security principles and practices. They act as advocates for security and help bridge the gap between security experts and other team members.

Security Champions play several vital roles:

1. **Education and Training**: They educate team members about security best practices, threats, and vulnerabilities. This includes conducting training sessions, sharing resources, and helping developers write more secure code.
2. **Security Reviews**: Champions participate in security reviews of code, infrastructure, and configurations. They provide valuable insights and guidance on security issues and potential solutions.
3. **Threat Modeling**: They assist in threat modeling exercises, identifying potential security risks in applications and infrastructure designs. By involving Security Champions early in the design phase, you can proactively address security concerns.
4. **Incident Response**: In the event of a security incident or breach, Security Champions help coordinate the response efforts, ensuring that the incident is properly handled and resolved.

Security as Code

Collaborative security practices promote the concept of "Security as Code." This means treating security policies, standards, and checks as code artifacts that can be version-controlled, automated, and integrated into your pipelines.

Policy as Code: Security policies can be defined as code using tools like Azure Policy or Open Policy Agent (OPA). These policies are enforced automatically, ensuring that resources in your Azure environment adhere to security requirements.

Infrastructure as Code (IaC) Security: Security checks can be integrated into your IaC templates. For example, you can use tools like Terrascan or Checkov to scan Terraform or ARM templates for security issues during the deployment process.

Code Scanning: Integrating code scanning tools such as static application security testing (SAST) and dynamic application security testing (DAST) into your pipelines allows you to identify and remediate security vulnerabilities in your applications.

Threat Modeling

Threat modeling is a proactive security practice that involves identifying potential threats and vulnerabilities in your applications and infrastructure. Collaborative threat modeling sessions bring together developers, security experts, and other stakeholders to assess security risks systematically.

During a threat modeling session:

1. **Identify Assets**: List the assets, components, and data that need protection, including APIs, databases, user data, and authentication mechanisms.
2. **Enumerate Threats**: Identify potential threats and vulnerabilities that could affect the assets. These threats can include data breaches, denial-of-service attacks, or unauthorized access.
3. **Assess Risks**: Evaluate the likelihood and impact of each threat. Prioritize risks based on their severity and potential consequences.
4. **Mitigation Strategies**: Collaboratively brainstorm and

document mitigation strategies for each identified risk. This may involve code changes, security controls, or architectural adjustments.

5. **Iterate and Review**: Continue to refine the threat model as the application evolves. Regular reviews ensure that new features and changes are assessed for security risks.

Secure DevOps Pipelines

Collaboration extends to the development of secure DevOps pipelines. Security experts, developers, and operations teams work together to define security controls, integrate security checks into the pipeline, and continuously monitor and improve security practices.

Key practices for secure DevOps pipelines include:

1. **Pipeline as Code**: Define your pipeline configurations as code, allowing you to version-control, audit, and test changes to your CI/CD process.
2. **Automated Security Checks**: Incorporate automated security checks into your pipelines, such as vulnerability scanning, security testing, and compliance checks.
3. **Secure Containerization**: Ensure that container images used in your pipelines are built securely, with minimal attack surfaces and up-to-date dependencies.
4. **Continuous Monitoring**: Implement continuous monitoring and alerting to detect and respond to security incidents in real-time.

Collaborative security practices empower teams to take collective ownership of security, making it an integral part of the development and delivery process. By fostering a culture of collaboration, education, and proactive security, organizations can build more resilient and secure software systems.

Section 16.5: Continuous Security Monitoring and Compliance

Continuous security monitoring and compliance are critical components of a robust DevSecOps strategy. In this section, we'll explore the importance of ongoing security monitoring and how to ensure compliance with security standards in your Azure DevOps environment.

The Need for Continuous Security Monitoring

Traditional security approaches often involve periodic security assessments and compliance checks, which may lead to delayed detection of security issues. In DevSecOps, the goal is to shift security left in the development process and maintain continuous vigilance to detect and respond to security threats promptly.

Continuous security monitoring offers several benefits:

1. **Real-time Threat Detection**: It enables the immediate detection of security threats, vulnerabilities, and suspicious activities within your Azure DevOps environment.
2. **Rapid Incident Response**: With continuous monitoring, security incidents can be detected and responded to quickly, minimizing potential damage.
3. **Compliance Assurance**: Continuous monitoring ensures ongoing compliance with security policies, standards, and regulations.
4. **Risk Reduction**: By identifying and addressing security issues as they arise, the overall risk to your applications and

infrastructure is reduced.

Implementing Continuous Security Monitoring

To establish continuous security monitoring in Azure DevOps, consider the following practices:

1. Automated Security Checks

Integrate automated security checks into your CI/CD pipelines. These checks should include static application security testing (SAST), dynamic application security testing (DAST), software composition analysis (SCA), and vulnerability scanning of container images. Automated checks provide real-time feedback to developers during the build and release process, enabling them to address security findings early.

2. Security Information and Event Management (SIEM)

Implement a Security Information and Event Management (SIEM) system to collect, correlate, and analyze security-related events and logs from your Azure DevOps environment. SIEM tools, such as Azure Sentinel, can help you detect and respond to security incidents in real-time. Create custom alerts and dashboards to monitor critical security events.

3. Continuous Compliance Monitoring

Define compliance baselines and use automated tools to monitor and enforce compliance with security standards and regulations. Azure Policy and Azure Security Center provide capabilities to assess and remediate non-compliant resources and configurations.

Regularly review compliance reports and address any issues promptly.

4. Threat Intelligence Feeds

Subscribe to threat intelligence feeds to stay informed about emerging threats and vulnerabilities relevant to your Azure DevOps environment. Integrate threat intelligence sources with your SIEM system to enhance threat detection capabilities.

5. User and Access Monitoring

Monitor user activities and access to Azure DevOps services. Implement role-based access control (RBAC) to ensure that users have the appropriate permissions. Set up alerts for unusual or unauthorized access patterns.

6. Intrusion Detection and Prevention

Deploy intrusion detection and prevention systems (IDS/IPS) to monitor network traffic and identify potential attacks or anomalies. These systems can help protect your Azure DevOps infrastructure from known and unknown threats.

Continuous Compliance Assurance

Ensuring compliance with security standards and regulations is an ongoing process. Here are key steps to maintain continuous compliance in your Azure DevOps environment:

1. Compliance Baselines

Establish clear compliance baselines that define the security requirements, configurations, and policies that must be adhered to within your organization.

2. Automated Auditing

Leverage automated auditing tools, such as Azure Policy, to assess and enforce compliance with your defined baselines. Regularly run compliance checks to identify non-compliant resources.

3. Remediation

Implement automated remediation processes to bring non-compliant resources back into compliance. Azure Policy's "remediation tasks" feature allows you to automatically fix configuration drift.

4. Continuous Monitoring

Continuously monitor your Azure DevOps resources and configurations for compliance. Set up alerts and notifications for any deviations from your compliance baselines.

5. Documentation and Reporting

Maintain detailed documentation of your compliance efforts, including audit trails, remediation actions, and compliance reports. Reporting is essential for demonstrating compliance to auditors and stakeholders.

6. Regular Review

Regularly review and update your compliance baselines to align with changing security standards and regulatory requirements.

Continuous security monitoring and compliance ensure that your Azure DevOps environment remains secure and compliant throughout the software development lifecycle. By integrating security into every phase of development and maintaining vigilant monitoring, you can proactively protect your applications and data from evolving threats.

Section 17.1: Mobile Development in Azure DevOps

Mobile application development is a vital part of modern software engineering, and Azure DevOps provides a comprehensive set of tools and services to support the development, testing, and deployment of mobile apps across various platforms. In this section, we'll explore how Azure DevOps can streamline mobile development processes, foster collaboration among development teams, and ensure the delivery of high-quality mobile applications.

Mobile Development Challenges

Mobile app development comes with unique challenges, such as multiple platforms (iOS, Android), device fragmentation, and the need for rapid updates and releases. Azure DevOps addresses these challenges with the following features and capabilities:

1. Cross-Platform Development

Azure DevOps supports cross-platform mobile development, allowing you to build applications that can run on both iOS and

Android. You can use popular frameworks like Xamarin, React Native, or Flutter to write code that works across platforms, saving time and effort.

2. Code Repositories

Azure Repos, a part of Azure DevOps, provides a robust version control system for managing your mobile app's source code. Whether you're working on a native iOS app in Swift, an Android app in Kotlin, or a cross-platform app, Azure Repos offers a secure and collaborative environment for code storage and versioning.

3. Continuous Integration and Deployment (CI/CD)

Implementing CI/CD pipelines for mobile apps is crucial for automating build, testing, and deployment processes. Azure Pipelines allows you to set up automated workflows to build, test, and distribute your mobile app to various app stores. This ensures that your app is always up-to-date and meets quality standards.

4. Mobile Testing

Azure DevOps provides tools for mobile app testing, including manual testing, automated UI testing, and performance testing. You can create test plans, track test cases, and automate testing across different devices and platforms to ensure your app functions as expected.

5. Mobile App Distribution

Distributing mobile apps to beta testers, stakeholders, or app stores is simplified with Azure DevOps. You can use distribution services like Visual Studio App Center (formerly HockeyApp) to manage app distribution, collect feedback, and monitor app usage.

6. Monitoring and Analytics

Once your mobile app is live, monitoring user behavior and app performance is critical. Azure Application Insights and other monitoring tools allow you to gain insights into how users interact with your app, identify issues, and make data-driven improvements.

7. Collaboration

Collaboration among cross-functional teams, including developers, designers, testers, and product managers, is essential for successful mobile app development. Azure DevOps offers collaborative tools and dashboards to facilitate communication, track progress, and manage work items efficiently.

Mobile DevOps Best Practices

To succeed in mobile app development with Azure DevOps, consider these best practices:

- **Automate Build and Testing**: Implement automated build and testing pipelines to catch issues early and ensure consistent app quality.

- **Embrace DevOps Principles**: Apply DevOps principles like continuous integration, continuous delivery, and collaboration to streamline your mobile development process.

- **Leverage Cross-Platform Development**: Choose a cross-platform framework that suits your project's needs to save time and resources.

- **Prioritize User Experience**: Focus on delivering a seamless user experience by regularly testing on real devices and addressing user feedback.
- **Monitor and Iterate**: Continuously monitor app performance, collect user feedback, and iterate on your app to deliver value to users.

With Azure DevOps, mobile app development teams can overcome challenges and build high-quality applications that meet user expectations and stay competitive in the rapidly evolving mobile landscape. Whether you're creating native or cross-platform mobile apps, Azure DevOps provides the tools and workflows to support your development journey.

Section 17.2: Cross-Platform Development Strategies

Cross-platform development is a popular approach for mobile app development, allowing developers to create applications that run on multiple operating systems, such as iOS and Android, using a single codebase. Azure DevOps supports cross-platform development by providing tools, services, and best practices that streamline the development process. In this section, we will explore various cross-platform development strategies and how Azure DevOps can assist in implementing them effectively.

Choosing a Cross-Platform Framework

The first step in cross-platform development is selecting a suitable framework that allows you to write code once and deploy it on multiple platforms. Some of the popular cross-platform frameworks include:

1. **Xamarin**: Xamarin is a Microsoft-owned framework that allows developers to write C# code and share it across iOS, Android, and Windows platforms. It provides a native-like experience and access to platform-specific APIs.
2. **React Native**: Developed by Facebook, React Native enables developers to build mobile apps using JavaScript and React. It offers a high degree of code reuse and a rich ecosystem of community-contributed components.
3. **Flutter**: Flutter is Google's open-source UI toolkit for building natively compiled applications for mobile, web, and desktop from a single codebase. It uses the Dart programming language and offers a fast and customizable user interface.
4. **PhoneGap/Cordova**: Apache Cordova (formerly known as PhoneGap) is a framework for building mobile apps using HTML, CSS, and JavaScript. It wraps the app in a WebView, providing access to device capabilities.
5. **Unity**: While primarily used for game development, Unity can also be used for creating interactive and visually rich cross-platform applications.

The choice of framework depends on factors such as the project's requirements, team expertise, and performance considerations. Azure DevOps supports all these frameworks, enabling teams to manage their cross-platform projects efficiently.

Azure DevOps for Cross-Platform Development

Azure DevOps provides several features and practices to support cross-platform development:

1. **Source Control**: Azure Repos allows teams to manage their cross-platform codebase, irrespective of the chosen

framework. Developers can collaborate on the same codebase, implement branching strategies, and ensure version control.

2. **Continuous Integration and Continuous Deployment (CI/CD)**: Azure Pipelines can automate the build, test, and deployment processes for cross-platform applications. Teams can configure CI/CD pipelines to build and package apps for multiple platforms, ensuring consistent builds and releases.
3. **Testing and Automation**: Azure DevOps offers a range of testing capabilities, including automated UI testing, unit testing, and performance testing. These can be integrated into the CI/CD pipeline to ensure the quality of the cross-platform app.
4. **Collaboration and Communication**: Cross-functional teams can use Azure DevOps boards and dashboards to track progress, manage work items, and communicate effectively. Agile methodologies can be implemented to manage the development process efficiently.
5. **Monitoring and Analytics**: Once the cross-platform app is deployed, Azure Application Insights and other monitoring tools can be used to gather data on app usage and performance across different platforms. This data-driven approach helps teams make informed decisions and improve the app.

Best Practices for Cross-Platform Development

To make the most of Azure DevOps for cross-platform development, consider the following best practices:

- **Select the Right Framework**: Choose a cross-platform framework that aligns with your project's goals, ensuring a balance between code reuse and platform-specific capabilities.

- **Automate Everything**: Automate as much of the development process as possible, from building and testing to deployment. This reduces manual errors and accelerates development.

- **Implement Code Sharing Strategies**: Leverage code sharing techniques within your chosen framework to maximize code reuse across platforms.

- **Device Testing**: Test your app on real devices to ensure compatibility and address platform-specific issues.

- **User Experience**: Pay special attention to the user experience on each platform. Users expect apps to feel native, so design and test accordingly.

- **Monitoring and Optimization**: Continuously monitor app performance and user feedback, and use this data to optimize the app on each platform.

By following these strategies and leveraging Azure DevOps tools and services, development teams can successfully build and maintain cross-platform mobile applications, reaching a broader audience and delivering value efficiently.

Section 17.3: Building and Deploying Mobile Apps

Building and deploying mobile apps, whether for iOS, Android, or other platforms, is a critical aspect of cross-platform development. In this section, we'll explore the process of building and deploying mobile apps using Azure DevOps, focusing on best practices and tools available to streamline this workflow.

Mobile App Development Workflow

The development of mobile apps typically follows a series of steps, including design, development, testing, and deployment. Azure DevOps supports each of these phases, helping teams manage the process efficiently:

1. **Design**: During the design phase, teams create wireframes, user interface (UI) designs, and user experience (UX) prototypes. Collaboration tools in Azure DevOps, such as boards and wikis, facilitate the design process and capture requirements.
2. **Development**: Developers write code for the mobile app using the chosen cross-platform framework (e.g., Xamarin, React Native, or Flutter). Azure Repos provides version control, enabling multiple team members to collaborate on the codebase. Code reviews and pull requests help maintain code quality.
3. **Testing**: Azure DevOps offers various testing tools and practices for mobile apps. Automated UI testing, unit testing, and performance testing can be integrated into the CI/CD pipeline to catch issues early. Testing on real devices is crucial to ensure compatibility.
4. **Continuous Integration and Continuous Deployment (CI/CD)**: Azure Pipelines automates the CI/CD process for mobile apps. It builds, tests, and packages the app for deployment. The CI/CD pipeline should be configured to target different platforms (iOS and Android) and app stores (e.g., Apple App Store and Google Play Store).

Deploying to App Stores

Deploying mobile apps to app stores is a pivotal step in making them available to users. Azure DevOps provides guidance and tools to help teams navigate this process smoothly:

Apple App Store (iOS)

For iOS apps, deploying to the Apple App Store involves several steps:

1. **App Distribution Profile**: Create an App Distribution Profile in Apple Developer Center to identify your app and configure its distribution.
2. **Certificates and Provisioning Profiles**: Generate distribution certificates and provisioning profiles for your app.
3. **App Store Connect**: Log in to App Store Connect and create an app listing, including metadata, screenshots, and app information.
4. **Azure Pipelines**: Configure your CI/CD pipeline to build and package the iOS app using the generated certificates and provisioning profiles. Use the "App Store Connect" task to upload the app to App Store Connect.
5. **Submission and Review**: Submit your app for review on the Apple App Store. Apple reviews the app for compliance with its guidelines.
6. **Release**: Once approved, release the app on the App Store for users to download.

Google Play Store (Android)

Deploying Android apps to the Google Play Store involves the following steps:

1. **Google Play Console**: Create an app listing on the Google Play Console, providing details about your app, including its title, description, and screenshots.
2. **Keystore**: Generate a keystore file that will be used to sign the Android app bundle (AAB) or APK.
3. **Azure Pipelines**: Configure your CI/CD pipeline to build and sign the Android app using the keystore. Package the app as an AAB or APK.
4. **Google Play Console**: Upload the signed AAB or APK to the Google Play Console and provide necessary metadata.
5. **Review and Release**: Google reviews the app and, once approved, allows you to release it to the Google Play Store for users to install.

Best Practices

To ensure a successful deployment of mobile apps using Azure DevOps, consider the following best practices:

• **Automate Everything**: Automate the build, test, and deployment processes to minimize manual errors and ensure consistency across platforms.

• **Testing on Real Devices**: Test the app on real devices to catch platform-specific issues and ensure a smooth user experience.

• **Versioning**: Use semantic versioning to manage app versions and updates.

- **Monitoring and Feedback**: Implement monitoring tools to gather user feedback and app performance data post-deployment. Use this feedback for continuous improvement.

- **Security**: Ensure that app packages are securely stored and distributed. Protect sensitive information, such as API keys and secrets.

By following these best practices and leveraging Azure DevOps tools and pipelines, development teams can effectively build and deploy cross-platform mobile apps, reaching a wider audience and delivering value to users on various devices and platforms.

Section 17.4: Testing Mobile Applications in Azure DevOps

Testing is a crucial part of mobile application development. It ensures that the app functions correctly, provides a good user experience, and is free from defects. Azure DevOps offers a comprehensive set of tools and practices for testing mobile applications, allowing development teams to catch and address issues early in the development process.

Types of Mobile App Testing

Before diving into the testing tools and practices, it's important to understand the various types of testing that are typically performed on mobile applications:

1. **Unit Testing**: Unit tests focus on individual components or functions within the code to verify their correctness. For mobile apps, this includes testing specific methods or

functions in the app's codebase.

2. **UI Testing**: UI tests ensure that the user interface of the app behaves as expected. Test scripts interact with the app's UI elements to validate their functionality and appearance.
3. **Integration Testing**: Integration tests examine how different components of the app work together. This can include testing the interaction between the app and external services or APIs.
4. **Functional Testing**: Functional tests verify that the app's features and functions work correctly. Test scenarios cover common user interactions and use cases.
5. **Performance Testing**: Performance testing assesses the app's responsiveness, stability, and resource usage under various conditions, such as different network speeds and device configurations.
6. **Compatibility Testing**: Compatibility tests ensure that the app works well on different devices, operating systems, and screen sizes. This is particularly important for cross-platform mobile development.

Azure DevOps Testing Tools and Practices

Azure DevOps provides a range of tools and practices to support mobile app testing:

1. Azure Test Plans: Azure Test Plans is a comprehensive testing solution that allows teams to plan, track, and manage test cases. It supports manual and automated testing, making it suitable for both UI and non-UI testing. Testers can create test cases, execute them, and log defects directly within Azure DevOps.

2. Azure Test Automation: For automated UI testing, Azure DevOps integrates with popular testing frameworks like Appium

and Xamarin.UITest. Teams can write test scripts that interact with the app's user interface to validate its functionality.

3. Emulators and Simulators: Azure DevOps allows teams to run tests on emulators and simulators to cover various device configurations and screen sizes without the need for physical devices.

4. Real Device Testing: To ensure real-world compatibility and performance, Azure DevOps supports running tests on physical devices. Teams can use cloud-based testing services like Xamarin Test Cloud (now part of App Center) to execute tests on a variety of real devices.

5. Performance Testing: Azure DevOps offers load testing capabilities to assess the app's performance under stress. Teams can simulate a large number of concurrent users and monitor the app's behavior.

6. Continuous Testing: Implementing continuous testing in the CI/CD pipeline ensures that tests are automatically executed whenever changes are made to the app's codebase. This helps catch regressions early.

7. Test Analytics: Azure DevOps provides test analytics and reporting, allowing teams to track test results, identify trends, and make data-driven decisions for improving the app's quality.

8. Device Clouds: Azure DevOps integrates with cloud-based device farms, such as Azure App Center Test, which provides access to a vast array of real devices for testing.

Best Practices for Mobile App Testing

To maximize the effectiveness of mobile app testing in Azure DevOps, consider the following best practices:

- **Automate Tests**: Automate as many tests as possible, especially regression tests, to save time and catch issues early.

- **Test on Real Devices**: Test on real devices to ensure accurate results and identify device-specific issues.

- **Integrate Testing into CI/CD**: Integrate testing into your CI/CD pipeline to automatically run tests with each code change.

- **Test Across Platforms**: If you're developing cross-platform apps, ensure testing across various platforms and versions.

- **Performance Testing**: Include performance testing to assess the app's responsiveness and resource usage under different conditions.

- **Regularly Update Tests**: Keep test scripts up-to-date as the app evolves to maintain test accuracy.

By following these practices and leveraging Azure DevOps testing tools, development teams can ensure the reliability and quality of their mobile applications, providing a better user experience and reducing the likelihood of post-release issues.

Section 17.5: Performance Monitoring for Mobile Apps

Performance monitoring is a critical aspect of mobile app development. It ensures that your app runs smoothly and efficiently, delivering a positive user experience. Azure DevOps provides tools and practices to monitor the performance of your mobile apps throughout their lifecycle.

Why Performance Monitoring Matters

Poor performance in a mobile app can lead to user frustration, negative reviews, and loss of users. Therefore, it's essential to monitor and optimize the following aspects of your mobile app's performance:

1. **Responsiveness**: Ensure that the app responds promptly to user interactions, such as taps and swipes.
2. **Load Times**: Minimize the time it takes for the app to load initially and retrieve data from servers.
3. **Battery Usage**: Optimize resource usage to prevent excessive battery drain on mobile devices.
4. **Network Efficiency**: Reduce the amount of data transferred over the network to minimize data costs and improve speed.
5. **Stability**: Detect and resolve crashes, freezes, or other stability issues that can disrupt the user experience.

Azure DevOps Performance Monitoring Tools

Azure DevOps offers several tools and practices to monitor the performance of your mobile apps:

1. Application Insights: Azure Application Insights is a powerful

tool for monitoring the performance and usage of your mobile apps. It provides real-time telemetry data, including user interactions, exceptions, and performance metrics. You can gain insights into how users are using your app and identify performance bottlenecks.

2. Crash Analytics: Azure DevOps integrates with crash analytics platforms like Microsoft App Center, which helps you track and prioritize crashes and exceptions in your app. This allows you to quickly identify and address issues that cause your app to crash.

3. User Analytics: Understanding user behavior is essential for optimizing app performance. Azure DevOps tools can provide insights into how users interact with your app, helping you make data-driven decisions to enhance performance.

4. Load Testing: Azure DevOps supports load testing to simulate user traffic and measure your app's performance under different loads. This helps identify potential bottlenecks and scalability issues.

5. Continuous Monitoring: Implement continuous monitoring in your CI/CD pipeline to automatically detect performance regressions with each code change. This proactive approach helps maintain consistent app performance.

6. Alerting: Set up alerts based on predefined performance thresholds. When performance issues are detected, Azure DevOps can notify your team, allowing you to take action promptly.

Best Practices for Performance Monitoring

To ensure effective performance monitoring for your mobile apps using Azure DevOps, consider the following best practices:

- **Instrument Your Code**: Properly instrument your code to collect performance data, including user interactions, exceptions, and resource usage.

- **Monitor in Real Time**: Monitor your app's performance in real-time to detect and address issues as they occur.

- **Use APM Tools**: Leverage Application Performance Monitoring (APM) tools to gain insights into your app's performance, bottlenecks, and user behavior.

- **Analyze and Optimize**: Regularly analyze performance data and use it to optimize your app. Focus on areas that have the most significant impact on user experience.

- **Automate Testing**: Integrate performance testing into your CI/CD pipeline to catch performance regressions early in the development process.

- **Collaborate Across Teams**: Ensure that developers, testers, and operations teams collaborate to identify and resolve performance issues effectively.

By following these best practices and leveraging Azure DevOps performance monitoring tools, you can proactively identify and address performance issues in your mobile apps, delivering a better user experience and ensuring the success of your mobile application.

Chapter 18: Leveraging AI and Machine Learning in Azure DevOps

Section 18.1: AI and ML Basics for DevOps

In recent years, the integration of Artificial Intelligence (AI) and Machine Learning (ML) in DevOps practices has gained significant attention. These technologies offer the potential to enhance various aspects of the DevOps lifecycle, from improving code quality to optimizing deployment processes. In this section, we'll explore the fundamentals of AI and ML and their relevance in the context of DevOps.

Understanding Artificial Intelligence (AI)

AI is a broad field of computer science that aims to create systems capable of performing tasks that typically require human intelligence. These tasks include natural language processing, problem-solving, decision-making, and pattern recognition. AI systems can be classified into two categories: narrow AI (or weak AI) and general AI (or strong AI).

- **Narrow AI**: Narrow AI refers to AI systems designed for specific tasks, such as virtual assistants, recommendation systems, and image recognition. These systems excel in their designated domains but lack general intelligence.

- **General AI**: General AI, on the other hand, refers to AI systems with human-like cognitive abilities, capable of understanding, learning, and adapting to various tasks and situations. General AI remains a theoretical concept and has not been achieved yet.

Exploring Machine Learning (ML)

Machine Learning is a subset of AI that focuses on developing algorithms and models that enable computers to learn from data and make predictions or decisions without explicit programming. ML algorithms can be categorized into three main types:

1. **Supervised Learning**: In supervised learning, models are trained on labeled data, meaning the input data is paired with corresponding output labels. The model learns to make predictions or classifications based on this labeled training data.
2. **Unsupervised Learning**: Unsupervised learning involves training models on unlabeled data to discover hidden patterns or structures within the data. Clustering and dimensionality reduction are common unsupervised learning tasks.
3. **Reinforcement Learning**: Reinforcement learning is concerned with training agents to make a sequence of decisions to maximize a reward. It is often used in scenarios where an agent interacts with an environment.

AI and ML Applications in DevOps

AI and ML can be applied at various stages of the DevOps lifecycle:

- **Code Analysis and Quality**: ML models can analyze code to identify potential issues, bugs, or vulnerabilities. They can also suggest code improvements and coding standards compliance.

- **Test Automation**: ML algorithms can improve test automation by predicting which tests to run based on code changes, reducing testing time and costs.

- **Release Management**: AI can optimize release planning and predict the impact of code changes on production systems, allowing for more accurate risk assessment.

- **Incident Detection and Response**: ML-based anomaly detection can identify unusual patterns in system metrics, helping to detect and respond to incidents proactively.

- **Predictive Analytics**: ML models can forecast resource utilization, application performance, and infrastructure needs, aiding in capacity planning.

- **Chatbots and Virtual Assistants**: AI-powered chatbots and virtual assistants can assist developers and operations teams by providing answers to common questions and automating routine tasks.

As organizations increasingly embrace DevOps practices, the integration of AI and ML technologies can provide a competitive advantage by enhancing efficiency, quality, and agility. Understanding the basics of AI and ML is the first step toward harnessing their potential in the world of DevOps. In the subsequent sections, we will delve deeper into practical applications and use cases of AI and ML in Azure DevOps.

Section 18.2: Integrating AI/ML Workflows in DevOps

In Section 18.1, we discussed the fundamentals of Artificial Intelligence (AI) and Machine Learning (ML) and their relevance to DevOps. Now, let's explore how AI/ML workflows can be seamlessly integrated into the DevOps processes to enhance efficiency and drive automation.

Data Collection and Preparation

AI/ML models heavily rely on data, and the first step in integrating AI/ML into DevOps is to gather and prepare the necessary data. This data may include code repositories, historical performance metrics, user behavior logs, and more. Data engineers and DevOps teams collaborate to ensure data is collected, cleaned, and stored appropriately.

Model Training and Development

Once the data is ready, data scientists and machine learning engineers come into play. They develop and train ML models using tools like TensorFlow, PyTorch, or scikit-learn. For DevOps purposes, models are often trained to address specific tasks, such as predicting code quality, optimizing resource allocation, or automating testing.

Model Deployment and Inference

After training, ML models need to be deployed in a way that makes them accessible to the DevOps pipeline. Containers and container orchestration platforms like Docker and Kubernetes are commonly used for this purpose. The models are deployed as microservices, making them available for real-time inference or batch processing.

Continuous Integration (CI) and Continuous Deployment (CD)

Integrating AI/ML into CI/CD pipelines is crucial for automating the deployment of models and ensuring that they are up-to-date. Whenever code changes trigger CI/CD processes, the corresponding ML models should also be retrained and deployed if necessary. This ensures that the AI/ML components are always aligned with the codebase.

```
# Example CI/CD YAML Configuration

stages:

- build

- test

- deploy

- train_ml_model

- deploy_ml_model
```

Monitoring and Feedback Loops

Monitoring AI/ML models in production is essential. DevOps teams use monitoring tools to track model performance, resource utilization, and potential issues. Feedback loops are established to retrain models with fresh data and continuously improve their accuracy and effectiveness.

A/B Testing and Experimentation

A/B testing is a common practice in DevOps and is equally applicable to AI/ML. DevOps teams can run experiments with multiple models to determine which one performs best in a given scenario. A/B testing helps in making data-driven decisions about which models to deploy or roll back.

```
# Example A/B Testing Python Code

if experiment_a_accuracy > experiment_b_accuracy:

deploy_model_a()

else:

deploy_model_b()
```

Auto-Scaling and Resource Optimization

AI/ML workloads can be resource-intensive. DevOps practices like auto-scaling and resource optimization become critical when dealing with ML workloads to ensure efficient resource utilization and cost-effectiveness.

Collaboration and Documentation

Collaboration between data scientists, ML engineers, and DevOps teams is paramount. Proper documentation of AI/ML workflows, model specifications, and deployment procedures is essential for ensuring smooth collaboration and knowledge transfer.

Security and Compliance

Security practices for AI/ML in DevOps should cover data privacy, model integrity, and vulnerability assessments. Compliance with regulatory requirements, such as GDPR, should also be considered when handling sensitive data.

Integrating AI/ML workflows into DevOps requires a coordinated effort among various teams and the adoption of tools and practices that support this integration. By doing so, organizations can leverage AI/ML to automate tasks, improve decision-making, and enhance the overall efficiency of their DevOps processes. In the following sections, we will delve into specific use cases and practical implementations of AI/ML in Azure DevOps.

Section 18.3: Automated Testing and Quality Assurance with AI

Automated testing is a cornerstone of DevOps, ensuring that code changes don't introduce regressions or bugs. In this section, we'll explore how Artificial Intelligence (AI) can be harnessed to enhance automated testing and quality assurance processes within DevOps pipelines.

Test Case Generation

AI-powered test case generation is revolutionizing testing practices. Machine learning models can analyze code changes and automatically generate test cases to cover new functionality or changes in existing code. This reduces the manual effort required for test case creation and ensures comprehensive test coverage.

```
# Example of AI-generated test case code

def test_new_feature():

input_data = generate_input_data()

expected_output = generate_expected_output()

result = run_new_feature(input_data)

assert result == expected_output
```

Test Execution and Validation

AI can assist in executing and validating test cases. AI-driven testing frameworks can identify patterns in test results, helping to identify intermittent failures and understand the root causes of issues. This enables quicker diagnosis and resolution of problems.

Test Data Management

AI can aid in generating and managing test data. ML models can create synthetic data that mimics real-world scenarios, ensuring that tests are performed under various conditions. This is particularly valuable when dealing with sensitive or limited data sources.

Anomaly Detection

AI-based anomaly detection can automatically identify unusual behaviors in applications during testing. DevOps teams can use anomaly detection to pinpoint potential issues early in the development cycle, leading to faster issue resolution and higher software quality.

Performance Testing

AI can optimize performance testing by simulating real user behavior and load patterns. Machine learning models can analyze application performance metrics and suggest optimizations, leading to better scalability and responsiveness.

```
# AI-driven performance testing configuration

performance_test:

load_pattern: AI-generated_load_pattern

analyze_metrics: AI-driven_performance_analysis
```

optimization_suggestions: AI-suggested_optimizations

Continuous Feedback and Improvement

AI can continuously analyze test results and provide feedback to development teams. It can highlight areas with frequent failures or quality issues, enabling teams to focus their efforts on improving those aspects of the application.

Test Environment Management

AI can assist in managing test environments by automating the provisioning and configuration of test infrastructure. This ensures that test environments are consistent and reproducible, reducing environment-related issues.

Root Cause Analysis

When test failures occur, AI can perform root cause analysis by examining code changes, test results, and system logs. This helps teams identify the specific changes that led to failures, expediting the debugging process.

Test Orchestration

AI-powered test orchestration can prioritize and schedule tests based on code changes and critical paths within the application. This optimizes test execution and ensures that the most relevant tests are run first.

Integration with CI/CD

Integrating AI-driven testing into CI/CD pipelines enhances the automation and efficiency of the testing process. AI models can trigger tests automatically when code changes are pushed, and they can also determine if changes meet quality criteria before deployment.

The integration of AI into automated testing and quality assurance processes is transforming DevOps by reducing manual effort, improving test coverage, and enhancing the overall quality of software. DevOps teams can leverage AI to deliver more reliable and resilient applications, ultimately leading to improved user experiences and faster time-to-market. In the following section, we will delve into AI-driven analytics and insights within the DevOps landscape.

Section 18.4: AI-Driven Analytics and Insights

In the world of DevOps, data is king. AI-driven analytics and insights play a pivotal role in harnessing the vast amount of data generated throughout the software development lifecycle. This section explores how Artificial Intelligence (AI) can be utilized to extract meaningful insights, enhance decision-making, and optimize DevOps processes.

Data Aggregation and Visualization

AI-powered tools can aggregate data from various sources, including code repositories, build and deployment pipelines, monitoring systems, and user feedback. Once collected, AI can generate interactive visualizations and dashboards that provide real-time insights into the health and performance of software projects.

```
# Example of AI-generated data visualization code

import matplotlib.pyplot as plt
```

```
def generate_project_dashboard(data):
# AI-based data aggregation and visualization logic
insights = ai_analyze_data(data)
# Plotting the insights
plt.figure(figsize=(10, 6))
plt.bar(insights.keys(), insights.values())
plt.title("Project Health Dashboard")
plt.xlabel("Metrics")
plt.ylabel("Values")
plt.show()
```

Predictive Analytics

AI can leverage historical data to make predictions about future events and issues. For example, it can predict the likelihood of a code deployment causing a production incident or estimate the time required to resolve specific types of issues. Predictive analytics helps teams proactively address potential challenges.

Root Cause Analysis

When incidents or problems occur in a DevOps environment, AI can perform root cause analysis by examining various data sources. It correlates events, code changes, configuration alterations, and system metrics to identify the underlying causes of issues. This accelerates troubleshooting and resolution.

Anomaly Detection

AI excels at identifying anomalies within vast datasets. It can automatically detect unusual patterns or behaviors in application logs, performance metrics, and user activity. Anomaly detection helps teams uncover hidden issues and security threats.

```
# Configuration for AI-driven anomaly detection

anomaly_detection:

algorithm: AI-based_anomaly_detection

threshold: 0.95

alert_notifications: Slack, Email
```

Quality Metrics and Trends

AI can continuously monitor code quality metrics, such as code complexity, test coverage, and adherence to coding standards. It identifies trends over time, helping development teams maintain and improve code quality as the project evolves.

Release Readiness Assessment

AI can assess the readiness of a software release for deployment. It considers factors like code stability, test coverage, and the absence of critical issues. AI-driven release assessments reduce the risk of deploying unstable or error-prone code to production.

User Behavior Analysis

AI can analyze user behavior and feedback to identify patterns and preferences. This information can inform feature development and prioritize user-requested enhancements. Understanding user behavior is crucial for creating software that meets customer needs.

Cost Optimization

AI can optimize cloud resource allocation and spending by analyzing usage patterns and recommending resource adjustments. This ensures that resources are allocated efficiently and cost-effectively.

Integration with ChatOps

AI-driven analytics can integrate with ChatOps platforms to provide real-time insights and recommendations directly to development and operations teams. Chatbots equipped with AI can answer questions, provide recommendations, and assist in issue resolution.

Continuous Improvement

The insights and recommendations generated by AI-driven analytics contribute to a culture of continuous improvement within DevOps teams. By leveraging data-driven decision-making, teams can iteratively enhance their processes, streamline workflows, and deliver higher-quality software.

In conclusion, AI-driven analytics and insights empower DevOps teams to make data-driven decisions, improve software quality, and optimize the entire software development lifecycle. By harnessing AI's capabilities, organizations can stay competitive in a rapidly evolving technology landscape. The next section will explore the future prospects of AI in DevOps, shedding light on emerging trends and possibilities.

Section 18.5: Future Prospects of AI in DevOps

The integration of Artificial Intelligence (AI) into DevOps practices is an evolving frontier with immense potential. As technology advances and AI capabilities continue to grow, there are several exciting prospects for the future of AI in DevOps.

Enhanced Automation

One of the most prominent prospects is the continued automation of DevOps processes through AI. AI-driven automation can handle routine tasks, such as code testing, deployment, and monitoring, with minimal human intervention. This not only accelerates development cycles but also reduces the risk of human errors.

```
# AI-powered automation script for code testing
def ai_automate_testing(code_changes):
# AI logic for automated testing
test_results = ai_run_tests(code_changes)
if all(test_results):
ai_deploy_changes(code_changes)
else:
ai_notify_developers(test_results)
```

Self-Healing Systems

AI has the potential to create self-healing systems in DevOps. When an issue or outage occurs, AI can automatically diagnose the problem, rollback changes if necessary, and implement corrective actions. This proactive approach minimizes downtime and service interruptions.

Predictive Maintenance

In the realm of infrastructure and cloud management, AI can predict when hardware or software components are likely to fail. By analyzing historical data and performance metrics, AI can schedule maintenance and replacements before critical failures occur, ensuring high availability.

AI-Driven ChatOps

ChatOps platforms enriched with AI capabilities will become more prevalent. Chatbots equipped with natural language processing (NLP) can facilitate communication, provide real-time updates, and offer intelligent recommendations to DevOps teams directly within collaboration tools like Slack and Microsoft Teams.

```
# ChatOps configuration with AI-powered chatbot

chatops:

platform: Slack

chatbot: AI-assistant-bot

enable_recommendations: true

integration_with_pipeline: true
```

Advanced Security

AI will play a crucial role in bolstering security within DevOps. AI-powered security tools can continuously monitor for vulnerabilities and threats, detect anomalous behavior, and automatically respond to security incidents in real-time.

AI-Enhanced Testing

Testing will see significant enhancements with AI. AI-driven testing tools can generate test cases, perform exploratory testing, and even predict areas of code that are most likely to have defects. This improves test coverage and overall software quality.

```
# AI-based test case generation script
def generate_ai_test_cases(api_spec):
# AI logic for generating test cases from API specifications
test_cases = ai_generate_tests(api_spec)
return test_cases
```

AI in Compliance and Governance

AI will aid organizations in maintaining compliance and governance standards. By continuously monitoring and auditing DevOps processes, AI can ensure adherence to industry regulations and internal policies.

Collaboration and Knowledge Sharing

AI can assist in knowledge sharing and collaboration by providing context-aware recommendations and suggesting relevant documentation or resources to team members. This fosters a culture of learning and knowledge exchange.

Ethical Considerations

As AI becomes more integrated into DevOps, ethical considerations surrounding AI use will gain prominence. Organizations will need to establish ethical guidelines and frameworks for AI usage to ensure fairness, transparency, and accountability.

Democratization of AI

The accessibility of AI tools and technologies will continue to grow. DevOps teams, regardless of their size or budget, will have access to AI-driven solutions, democratizing the benefits of AI in software development and operations.

In conclusion, the future of AI in DevOps holds tremendous promise. It will reshape how DevOps teams operate, automate routine tasks, enhance security, and improve overall software quality. Embracing AI in DevOps is not merely a trend; it's a strategic imperative for organizations seeking to stay competitive and innovative in the ever-evolving technology landscape. This concludes the exploration of AI in DevOps, but the journey of discovery and implementation is ongoing, and the possibilities are limitless.

Chapter 19: Managing Data and Databases in Azure DevOps

Section 19.1: Database Management in DevOps

Managing databases in the context of DevOps presents unique challenges and opportunities. Databases are integral components of most applications, and their proper management is crucial for maintaining the reliability and performance of the software. This section explores the various aspects of database management within the DevOps lifecycle.

Database as Code

One of the fundamental principles of DevOps is treating infrastructure as code (IaC), and the same concept applies to databases. Database as Code (DaC) involves defining database schemas, configurations, and migrations in code. Tools like SQL scripts, database migration frameworks, and Infrastructure as Code (IaC) templates can be used to achieve this.

—Example of a SQL script defining a database table

```
CREATE TABLE Users (
UserID INT PRIMARY KEY,
Username VARCHAR(255) NOT NULL,
Email VARCHAR(255) UNIQUE
);
```

Continuous Integration for Databases

In DevOps, Continuous Integration (CI) extends to database changes. Developers can commit database schema changes as code, and CI pipelines automatically build and test these changes. This ensures that any database-related issues are identified early in the development cycle.

```
# CI pipeline configuration for database changes

stages:

- name: Build and Test

jobs:

- name: Build and Test Database

steps:

- checkout: self

- script: |

# Build and test database changes

db-migrate-tool build-and-test
```

Database Versioning

Version control systems play a crucial role in database management. Every database change should be versioned, allowing teams to track changes, roll back to previous states if necessary, and collaborate effectively. Git and other version control systems can be used for database versioning.

```
Database/
```

```
│
├── Schema/
│ ├── v1/
│ │ └── schema.sql
│ ├── v2/
│ │ └── schema.sql
│ └── ...
│
├── Data/
│ ├── v1/
│ │ └── initial_data.sql
│ ├── v2/
│ │ └── sample_data.sql
│ └── ...
│
├── Migrations/
│ ├── 20220101_create_users_table.sql
│ ├── 20220215_add_email_to_users.sql
│ └── ...
│
```

└── ...

Database CI/CD Pipelines

Implementing Continuous Deployment (CD) for databases involves creating automated pipelines that deploy database changes to various environments (e.g., development, staging, production). These pipelines should include thorough testing and validation steps.

```
# CD pipeline for database deployment

stages:

- name: Deploy to Staging

jobs:

- name: Deploy Database to Staging

steps:

- checkout: self

- script: |

# Deploy database changes to staging environment

db-migrate-tool deploy—environment=staging
```

Data Security and Compliance

Ensuring data security and compliance is paramount in database management. DevOps teams must implement access controls, encryption, and auditing to protect sensitive data. Compliance with regulations like GDPR or HIPAA may require specific configurations and practices.

Monitoring and Optimizing Database Performance

Continuous monitoring of database performance is essential. DevOps teams should leverage monitoring tools and practices to identify performance bottlenecks, optimize queries, and ensure that the database can handle the application's workload.

In summary, database management in DevOps involves treating databases as code, implementing CI/CD for database changes, versioning databases, ensuring data security and compliance, and continuously monitoring and optimizing database performance. Proper database management is essential for delivering reliable and performant applications in a DevOps environment.

Section 19.2: Implementing Database CI/CD Pipelines

Implementing Database Continuous Integration and Continuous Deployment (CI/CD) pipelines is a crucial aspect of managing data and databases in a DevOps environment. These pipelines automate the process of deploying database changes across different environments while ensuring consistency, reliability, and traceability. In this section, we'll explore the key concepts and practices for implementing robust CI/CD pipelines for databases.

Benefits of Database CI/CD

Database CI/CD pipelines offer several benefits:

1. **Automated Deployments:** Manual database deployments are error-prone and time-consuming. CI/CD pipelines automate the deployment process, reducing the risk of human errors.
2. **Consistency:** CI/CD ensures that database changes are

consistently applied to different environments, such as development, testing, staging, and production.

3. **Version Control:** Database changes are versioned and tracked, enabling rollbacks to previous states if issues arise.
4. **Testing and Validation:** CI/CD pipelines can include thorough testing and validation steps to catch errors early in the deployment process.
5. **Collaboration:** Teams can collaborate effectively by sharing code changes related to database schemas and configurations through version control.

CI/CD Pipeline Stages

A typical database CI/CD pipeline consists of the following stages:

1. **Build:** In the build stage, database changes (e.g., SQL scripts, schema modifications) are compiled and validated. This ensures that changes are syntactically correct and conform to best practices.

```
# Example build stage in a CI/CD pipeline

stages:

- name: Build

jobs:

- name: Build Database

steps:

- checkout: self

- script: |
```

Compile and validate database changes

db-migrate-tool build

1. **Test:** After building, the pipeline runs tests to verify that the database changes don't introduce regressions or compatibility issues with the application.

 # Example test stage in a CI/CD pipeline

stages:

- name: Test

jobs:

- name: Test Database

steps:

- checkout: self

- script: |

Run database tests

db-migrate-tool test

1. **Deploy:** The deploy stage is responsible for deploying the validated database changes to the target environment. This stage may involve creating backup copies, executing migration scripts, and applying configurations.

 # Example deploy stage in a CI/CD pipeline

stages:

- name: Deploy

jobs:

- name: Deploy Database

steps:

- checkout: self

- script: |

Deploy database changes to the target environment

db-migrate-tool deploy—environment=production

1. **Validation:** After deployment, the pipeline performs validation tests to ensure that the database changes are correctly applied and that the application functions as expected.

 # Example validation stage in a CI/CD pipeline

stages:

- name: Validation

jobs:

- name: Validate Deployment

steps:

- checkout: self

- script: |

Perform validation tests on the deployed database

db-validation-tool validate—environment=production

1. **Monitoring:** Monitoring and alerting are crucial components of a CI/CD pipeline. DevOps teams should set up monitoring tools to track database performance and identify issues in real-time.
2. **Rollback (Optional):** In case of critical issues or failures, a rollback stage can be included to revert the database changes to a previous state.

Tools for Database CI/CD

There are various tools available for implementing database CI/CD pipelines, such as:

• **Azure DevOps Pipelines:** Azure DevOps provides a robust platform for building and customizing CI/CD pipelines. It integrates seamlessly with other Azure services and can be used to deploy databases to Azure SQL Database or other platforms.

• **Jenkins:** Jenkins is a popular open-source automation server that can be configured to implement CI/CD for databases. It offers flexibility and extensibility through plugins.

• **CircleCI:** CircleCI is a cloud-based CI/CD platform that supports database deployments as part of its workflows. It allows you to define custom pipelines using configuration files.

• **Database-Specific Tools:** Some database management systems, like PostgreSQL and SQL Server, offer built-in support for CI/CD. Tools like Flyway and Liquibase are popular for managing database migrations and versioning.

In conclusion, implementing robust CI/CD pipelines for databases is essential for efficient and reliable database management in a DevOps environment. These pipelines automate the deployment process, ensuring consistency, version control, and thorough testing. Various tools are available to facilitate database CI/CD, allowing teams to choose the one that best fits their requirements and preferences.

Section 19.3: Database Versioning and Rollbacks

Database versioning and rollbacks are critical aspects of managing data and databases in a DevOps environment. Versioning ensures that changes made to the database schema and data are tracked, enabling teams to maintain a historical record and facilitating rollbacks in case issues arise. In this section, we'll explore the importance of database versioning and how to perform rollbacks effectively.

Database Versioning

Database versioning involves keeping track of changes to the database schema, stored procedures, triggers, and other database objects. Each change is assigned a version number or identifier, allowing teams to identify and manage different states of the database.

Version Control Systems

One of the fundamental tools for database versioning is a Version Control System (VCS) or Source Control System. Popular VCS options include Git, Subversion (SVN), and Mercurial. These systems enable teams to:

- **Commit Changes:** Developers can commit database scripts and schema changes to the VCS, which creates a historical record of modifications.

- **Branching and Merging:** Teams can create branches for different features or environments and merge changes as needed.

- **Conflict Resolution:** VCS systems provide mechanisms for resolving conflicts when multiple developers are working on the same database.

Database Migration Tools

Database migration tools like Flyway and Liquibase are specifically designed for managing database versioning. These tools work alongside VCS systems to apply and track database changes. They offer features such as:

- **Repeatable Migrations:** Code that should be executed only once, like creating reference data, can be defined as repeatable migrations.

- **Versioning:** Each migration script has a version number, allowing tools to determine which scripts need to be applied to reach a specific state of the database.

- **Rollbacks:** Database migration tools often provide rollback capabilities, enabling you to revert to a previous state of the database if issues occur.

Performing Rollbacks

Rollbacks are essential for reverting a database to a previous state in case of errors, failed deployments, or unexpected issues. Properly managing rollbacks ensures data integrity and system stability. Here are some best practices for performing rollbacks:

Automated Rollbacks

Whenever possible, rollbacks should be automated as part of the CI/CD pipeline. Automated rollbacks ensure consistency and reduce the risk of human errors during the rollback process.

```
# Example rollback stage in a CI/CD pipeline

stages:

- name: Rollback

jobs:

- name: Rollback Database

steps:

- checkout: self

- script: |

# Perform automated rollback to a previous state

db-migrate-tool rollback—version=1
```

Backups

Regularly creating database backups is a crucial part of rollback strategies. Backups should be taken before applying any changes to the database. In case of issues, you can restore the database to a known good state.

Rollback Plans

Developers and DevOps teams should create well-documented rollback plans that outline the steps required to revert changes. These plans should be tested in non-production environments to ensure their effectiveness.

Monitoring and Alerts

Implementing monitoring and alerting for database deployments is essential. If issues occur, the monitoring system can trigger alerts, and the rollback plan can be executed promptly.

Rollback Testing

Rollback procedures should be thoroughly tested in a controlled environment. Testing rollbacks helps identify any issues with the process and ensures that teams are prepared to execute them when needed.

In conclusion, database versioning and rollbacks are vital components of database management in a DevOps environment. Versioning allows teams to track and manage changes, while rollbacks ensure the ability to revert to a previous database state when necessary. Properly implementing version control systems, database migration tools, and rollback plans contributes to the stability and reliability of database deployments.

Section 19.4: Data Security and Compliance in DevOps

Data security and compliance are paramount concerns when managing data and databases in a DevOps environment. Organizations need to ensure that sensitive data is protected, and regulatory requirements are met. In this section, we will explore strategies and best practices for maintaining data security and compliance within DevOps pipelines.

Securing Sensitive Data

Encryption

Data should be encrypted both at rest and in transit. Utilizing encryption protocols such as TLS/SSL for data in transit and technologies like Transparent Data Encryption (TDE) or database encryption for data at rest helps safeguard sensitive information.

Access Control

Implement robust access control mechanisms to restrict access to databases. Role-based access control (RBAC) and permissions should be defined, granting access only to authorized personnel. Regularly review and update access control policies.

—Example SQL Server query to create a new user with specific permissions

CREATE LOGIN [username] **WITH PASSWORD** = 'password';

CREATE USER [username] **FOR** LOGIN [username];

GRANT SELECT, **INSERT**, **UPDATE**, **DELETE ON** [dbo].[TableName] **TO** [username];

Secrets Management

Use secure methods for storing and managing secrets, such as API keys, database credentials, and encryption keys. Azure Key Vault or HashiCorp Vault can be integrated into DevOps pipelines to store and retrieve secrets securely.

 # Example of storing a secret in Azure Key Vault

az keyvault secret set—name MySecret—value MySecretValue—vault-name MyKeyVault

Compliance Requirements

Regulatory Compliance

Different industries and regions have specific data compliance regulations, such as GDPR, HIPAA, or PCI DSS. DevOps teams must ensure that their database management practices align with these regulations. Implement auditing and monitoring to track compliance.

 # Example Azure Policy for auditing compliance

- policyRule:

if:

field: "Microsoft.Sql/servers/databases/auditingSettings.isComplianceAuditOn" equals: "False"

then:

effect: "deny"

details:

type: "AuditIfNotExists"

existenceCondition:

field: "Microsoft.Sql/servers/databases/auditingSettings.isComplianceAuditOn"

Data Masking and Anonymization

In non-production environments, it is advisable to mask or anonymize sensitive data to prevent unauthorized access. Tools like SQL Data Masking and third-party solutions can help automate this process.

—Example SQL Server query for data masking

ALTER TABLE [TableName] **ALTER COLUMN** [SensitiveColumn] **ADD** MASKED **WITH** (**FUNCTION** = 'partial(3,"XXX",0)');

Auditing and Logging

Implement robust auditing and logging mechanisms to track changes, access, and security-related events in databases. Centralized logging solutions like Azure Monitor and Azure Security Center can provide real-time insights and alerts.

// **Example Azure Policy for auditing database events**

```
{
"if": {
"field": "Microsoft.Sql/servers/databases/auditingSettings.isAuditEnabled",
"equals": "False"
},
"then": {
"effect": "audit",
"details": {
"type": "Microsoft.Sql/servers/databases/auditingSettings.isAuditEnabled",
"existenceCondition": {
"field": "Microsoft.Sql/servers/databases/auditingSettings.isAuditEnabled",
"equals": "False"
}
}
}
}
```

Continuous Compliance

DevOps teams should integrate compliance checks into their CI/CD pipelines. Automated testing and validation scripts can assess whether the database meets compliance requirements before deployment.

```
# Example CI/CD pipeline stage for compliance checks

stages:

- name: Compliance Checks

jobs:

- name: Run Compliance Tests

steps:

- checkout: self

- script: |

# Run compliance tests and validation scripts

db-compliance-test-tool run
```

In summary, data security and compliance are essential aspects of database management in DevOps. Encryption, access control, secrets management, and compliance checks should be integrated into the DevOps pipeline. Meeting regulatory requirements, data masking, and auditing ensure that sensitive data is protected, and organizations remain in compliance with applicable laws and regulations. Continuous monitoring and automation help maintain a secure and compliant database environment.

Section 19.5: Monitoring and Optimizing Database Performance

Continuous monitoring and performance optimization are critical aspects of managing databases in a DevOps environment. In this section, we will explore strategies and best practices for monitoring and optimizing the performance of your databases.

Database Performance Monitoring

Metrics and Alerts

Implement robust monitoring solutions to track database performance metrics such as CPU usage, memory utilization, query execution times, and storage consumption. Set up alerts to be notified of anomalies or performance degradation.

—Example SQL Server query to retrieve CPU usage

SELECT * **FROM** sys.dm_os_performance_counters **WHERE** counter_name = 'CPU usage %';

Query Performance

Regularly review and optimize database queries. Identify slow-performing queries and use tools like SQL Server Query Store or Azure SQL Database Query Performance Insight to analyze query execution plans and make improvements.

—Example SQL query to find top 10 slowest queries

SELECT TOP 10 query_text, average_duration

FROM sys.dm_exec_query_stats

ORDER BY average_duration **DESC**;

Indexing and Optimization

Index Maintenance

Regularly perform index maintenance tasks such as rebuilding or reorganizing indexes to ensure optimal query performance. Automated scripts and tools can help schedule and execute these tasks.

—Example SQL Server query to rebuild an index

ALTER INDEX [IndexName] **ON** [TableName] **REBUILD**;

Query Optimization

Use database query optimization techniques like indexing, partitioning, and query rewriting to enhance query performance. Consider denormalization for specific scenarios to reduce joins and improve response times.

—Example SQL Server query with query hint

SELECT * **FROM** [TableName] **WITH** (**INDEX**([IndexName]));

Scalability and Resource Management

Vertical Scaling

Consider vertical scaling by upgrading the hardware or resources of your database server to handle increased workloads. Monitor resource utilization and scale up when needed.

Horizontal Scaling

Explore horizontal scaling options like sharding or partitioning to distribute data across multiple databases or instances. Load balancing and connection pooling can help manage connections efficiently.

Automation and DevOps Integration

Continuous Monitoring

Integrate continuous monitoring into your CI/CD pipelines to ensure that changes in code or configurations do not negatively impact database performance. Tools like Azure Application Insights and SQL Database Advisor can assist in this regard.

```
# Example Azure DevOps pipeline stage for performance testing
stages:
- name: Performance Testing
jobs:
- name: Run Performance Tests
steps:
- checkout: self
- script: |
# Run performance tests and collect metrics
performance-test-tool run
```

Performance as Code

Treat database performance as code by storing performance-related configurations and optimizations in version control. This ensures that performance enhancements are part of the DevOps process.

```
# Example configuration file for database performance settings

performance:

queryTimeout: 5000

maxConnections: 100

indexingStrategy: 'auto'
```

Disaster Recovery and High Availability

Implement disaster recovery and high availability strategies to minimize downtime and maintain performance during failures. Solutions like Azure SQL Database Geo-Replication and Always On Availability Groups can help achieve this.

In conclusion, monitoring and optimizing database performance is an ongoing process in DevOps. By proactively monitoring key metrics, optimizing queries, managing indexes, and considering scalability options, organizations can ensure that their databases perform efficiently. Integrating performance testing into CI/CD pipelines and treating performance as code are essential practices for maintaining optimal database performance in a DevOps environment. Additionally, implementing disaster recovery and high availability measures is crucial to ensure business continuity in the event of failures.

Chapter 20: Conclusion and Future Directions

In this final chapter, we wrap up our journey through Azure DevOps and explore the future directions of DevOps and its integration with Azure services. We'll summarize key takeaways, discuss the evolving landscape of DevOps and Azure, provide resources for continuing education, offer career-building insights, and share some concluding thoughts.

Section 20.1: Summarizing Key Learnings in Azure DevOps

Let's begin by summarizing the key learnings and important takeaways from this comprehensive guide to Azure DevOps.

1. **DevOps Fundamentals**: We've covered the fundamental principles of DevOps, emphasizing collaboration, automation, and continuous improvement.
2. **Azure DevOps Services**: You've gained insights into Azure DevOps Services and its various components, including Azure Boards, Repos, Pipelines, Test Plans, and Artifacts.
3. **Infrastructure as Code (IaC)**: We explored IaC using Azure Resource Manager templates and integrating them into Azure DevOps pipelines.
4. **Security and Compliance**: Understanding security best practices, secrets management, and compliance within Azure DevOps is essential.
5. **Monitoring and Performance**: You've learned how to implement monitoring, performance optimization, and proactive alerting strategies.

6. **Customization and Extensibility**: We discussed customizing Azure DevOps using APIs, extensions, and automation tools.
7. **Scaling for Enterprises**: Managing Azure DevOps at enterprise scale and addressing security and compliance challenges were covered in detail.
8. **Migration and Integration**: Strategies for migrating to Azure DevOps from other platforms and integrating with third-party tools were explored.
9. **DevSecOps**: You've gained insights into integrating security practices into DevOps pipelines.
10. **Specialized Topics**: Topics like mobile development, AI/ML, database management, and more were touched upon.

The Future Landscape of DevOps and Azure

The world of DevOps is continually evolving, and Azure is at the forefront of these changes. Here are some future directions and trends to watch out for:

- **Kubernetes and Containers**: Kubernetes and containerization technologies will play a more significant role in DevOps workflows, and Azure Kubernetes Service (AKS) will continue to evolve.

- **Serverless Computing**: Azure Functions and other serverless offerings will become increasingly popular for building and deploying applications with minimal infrastructure management.

- **AI and Automation**: AI-driven automation will become more prevalent, aiding in tasks such as code reviews, testing, and deployment.

- **Edge Computing**: Azure's edge computing solutions will enable the deployment of applications closer to end-users, opening new possibilities for DevOps.

- **Hybrid Cloud**: DevOps practices will continue to focus on hybrid cloud solutions, bridging on-premises and cloud environments seamlessly.

Continuing Education and Resources

DevOps is a dynamic field, and continuous learning is crucial. Here are some resources to help you stay updated:

- **Online Courses**: Platforms like Coursera, edX, and Pluralsight offer DevOps-related courses.

- **Certifications**: Consider certifications like Microsoft Certified: Azure DevOps Engineer Expert, which validate your DevOps skills.

- **Conferences and Webinars**: Attend industry conferences, webinars, and meetups to network and learn from experts.

- **DevOps Blogs and Books**: Follow DevOps blogs and read books authored by experts in the field.

Building a Career in Azure DevOps

If you're considering a career in Azure DevOps, keep the following tips in mind:

1. **Continuous Learning**: Stay updated with the latest Azure and DevOps technologies.

2. **Certifications**: Achieve relevant certifications to validate your expertise.
3. **Hands-On Experience**: Gain practical experience through projects and hands-on practice.
4. **Networking**: Build a professional network by attending events and connecting with peers.
5. **Problem-Solving Skills**: Develop strong problem-solving and troubleshooting abilities.
6. **Soft Skills**: Effective communication, teamwork, and adaptability are essential skills.

Final Thoughts and Encouragement for DevOps Practitioners

As we conclude this journey through Azure DevOps, remember that DevOps is not just a set of tools or practices; it's a culture of collaboration and continuous improvement. Embrace change, be adaptable, and never stop learning. Azure DevOps provides a powerful platform to enable your DevOps journey, and with the right mindset and knowledge, you can contribute to the success of your organization's software development and delivery efforts.

Thank you for joining us on this exploration of Azure DevOps, and we wish you the very best in your DevOps endeavors.

Section 20.2: The Future Landscape of DevOps and Azure

In this section, we delve deeper into the evolving landscape of DevOps and Azure, exploring the trends and technologies that are shaping the future of software development and operations.

Kubernetes and Containers

One of the most significant trends in DevOps is the adoption of containerization and orchestration technologies like Kubernetes. Kubernetes has emerged as a de facto standard for container orchestration, and Azure provides robust support for Kubernetes through Azure Kubernetes Service (AKS). With AKS, DevOps teams can easily manage and scale containerized applications, making it a pivotal technology in the future of DevOps on Azure.

Containers offer several advantages, such as consistency across environments, rapid deployment, and efficient resource utilization. They enable developers to package applications and their dependencies into portable units that can run consistently in different environments, from development laptops to production clusters. Azure's support for Docker containers and Kubernetes allows teams to build, deploy, and scale containerized applications seamlessly.

Serverless Computing

Serverless computing is another area that is transforming the way applications are developed and deployed. Azure Functions, Azure's serverless computing offering, enables developers to write code that runs in response to events without worrying about the underlying infrastructure. This serverless approach simplifies application development and reduces operational overhead, making it an attractive choice for DevOps teams.

With serverless computing, developers can focus on writing code and delivering value to users while Azure takes care of the scaling, patching, and management of the underlying resources. This trend is expected to grow, and we can anticipate more serverless offerings and integration points within Azure DevOps pipelines.

AI and Automation

Artificial intelligence (AI) and automation are poised to play a more significant role in DevOps workflows. AI can be used to analyze code, identify potential issues, and even automate aspects of code review. Automated testing, performance monitoring, and security scanning can benefit from AI-driven solutions that can provide insights and recommendations in real-time.

Azure DevOps may integrate more AI-driven capabilities, such as automated release validation and intelligent error detection. These advancements can help reduce manual efforts and enhance the reliability and efficiency of DevOps processes.

Edge Computing

Edge computing, which involves processing data closer to the source of data generation or consumption, is an emerging trend that impacts DevOps practices. Azure offers solutions like Azure IoT Edge and Azure Stack Edge, which enable the deployment of applications at the edge. DevOps teams need to adapt their workflows to manage and deploy applications to edge locations efficiently.

As edge computing becomes more prevalent in industries like IoT and telecommunications, DevOps practices will need to address the challenges of managing distributed and resource-constrained environments.

Hybrid Cloud

Hybrid cloud solutions, which combine on-premises data centers with public cloud services, are becoming a standard approach for many organizations. DevOps practices must cater to hybrid cloud scenarios, ensuring seamless integration between on-premises and

Azure-based resources. Azure Arc, for example, allows organizations to manage on-premises and multi-cloud environments using Azure DevOps practices.

The ability to manage and deploy applications consistently across hybrid environments is crucial for DevOps teams. Strategies for maintaining consistency, security, and compliance will continue to evolve in this context.

These are just a few of the trends shaping the future of DevOps and Azure. DevOps practitioners should stay informed about these developments and be prepared to adapt their practices and toolsets to harness the full potential of these technologies. The ability to embrace change and leverage emerging technologies will be a key factor in the success of DevOps initiatives on Azure.

Section 20.3: Continuing Education and Resources

In this final section of the book, we focus on the importance of continuing education in the field of Azure DevOps, provide guidance on available resources, and offer advice for building a successful career in this dynamic and evolving domain.

Lifelong Learning

Azure DevOps, like the broader field of DevOps itself, is continuously evolving. New tools, technologies, and best practices emerge regularly. Therefore, it's crucial for professionals to commit to lifelong learning to stay relevant and advance their careers. Here are some strategies for ongoing education:

1. **Certifications:** Microsoft offers a range of Azure-related certifications, including those specific to Azure DevOps.

Pursuing these certifications can help validate your skills and knowledge. Examples include the Azure DevOps Engineer Expert certification and the Azure Administrator Associate certification.

2. **Online Courses and Tutorials:** Platforms like Microsoft Learn, Pluralsight, Coursera, and edX offer online courses and tutorials on Azure DevOps and related topics. These platforms provide both free and paid resources for self-paced learning.
3. **Books and Documentation:** Keep up to date with books, official documentation, and whitepapers related to Azure DevOps and Azure services. These resources provide in-depth insights and guidance on various topics.
4. **Conferences and Webinars:** Attend industry conferences, webinars, and meetups to learn from experts, network with peers, and stay informed about the latest trends and technologies.
5. **Community Engagement:** Participate in online communities, forums, and social media groups focused on Azure DevOps. Engaging with the community can provide valuable insights and opportunities for collaboration.

Azure DevOps Blogs and Podcasts

Blogs and podcasts are excellent sources of information and insights into Azure DevOps and DevOps practices in general. Consider following and subscribing to relevant blogs and podcasts to stay updated and gain valuable knowledge. Some notable Azure DevOps-related blogs and podcasts include:

- Azure DevOps Blog: The official Azure DevOps blog from Microsoft, providing announcements, tutorials, and best practices.

• DevOpsRadio: A podcast that covers various DevOps-related topics, including Azure DevOps.

• The DevOps Lab: A Microsoft Channel 9 show with video tutorials and discussions on Azure DevOps and related technologies.

• Donovan Brown's Blog[1]: Donovan Brown, Principal DevOps Manager at Microsoft, shares insights and tips on Azure DevOps and DevOps practices.

Building a Career in Azure DevOps

Building a successful career in Azure DevOps requires more than technical skills. Here are some key aspects to consider:

1. **Soft Skills:** Effective communication, collaboration, problem-solving, and leadership skills are essential in DevOps roles. Develop these skills to excel in your career.
2. **Domain Knowledge:** Gain a deep understanding of the domains you work in, such as software development, infrastructure, security, or databases, depending on your role and interests.
3. **Automation Mastery:** Proficiency in automation tools and scripting languages is a must. The ability to automate repetitive tasks and workflows is a valuable asset.
4. **Continuous Improvement:** Embrace the DevOps culture of continuous improvement. Seek feedback, learn from failures, and continually refine your processes.
5. **Stay Current:** Keep abreast of industry trends, best practices, and emerging technologies. Adapt to changes and be willing to explore new approaches.

1. https://donovanbrown.com/

6. **Certifications:** Consider obtaining relevant certifications to enhance your credentials and demonstrate your expertise to potential employers.
7. **Networking:** Build a professional network by attending conferences, joining online communities, and connecting with peers and mentors.

Final Thoughts

Azure DevOps is a dynamic and rapidly evolving field that offers exciting opportunities for professionals who are passionate about improving software delivery processes. By staying committed to learning, leveraging available resources, and cultivating essential skills, you can build a rewarding career in Azure DevOps and contribute to the success of your organization. Remember that DevOps is not just a set of tools; it's a cultural and philosophical shift that values collaboration, automation, and continuous improvement. Embrace these principles, and you'll be well on your way to success in the world of Azure DevOps.

Section 20.4: Building a Career in Azure DevOps

Building a successful career in Azure DevOps is an exciting journey that involves continuous learning, skill development, and career advancement. In this section, we'll explore the key aspects of establishing and nurturing a fulfilling career in the world of Azure DevOps.

Choosing Your Career Path

Azure DevOps offers a wide range of roles and career paths, depending on your interests and expertise. Here are some common career paths within Azure DevOps:

1. **Azure DevOps Engineer:** This role focuses on implementing and managing Azure DevOps tools and pipelines, ensuring the smooth flow of code from development to deployment.
2. **Software Developer:** Software developers in Azure DevOps work on developing, testing, and maintaining software applications. They often collaborate closely with DevOps engineers to streamline the delivery process.
3. **Cloud Engineer:** Cloud engineers specialize in managing cloud infrastructure, including Azure services. They work on infrastructure as code (IaC) and ensure the scalability and reliability of cloud environments.
4. **Security Engineer:** Security engineers focus on integrating security practices into the DevOps pipeline. They are responsible for identifying and mitigating security risks in applications and infrastructure.
5. **Site Reliability Engineer (SRE):** SREs concentrate on maintaining high availability, performance, and reliability of applications. They use automation and monitoring tools to ensure service uptime.
6. **Data Engineer:** Data engineers work on data pipelines, data warehousing, and data analytics in Azure environments. They play a crucial role in managing and optimizing data-related processes.

Skill Development

To excel in your chosen career path, continuous skill development is essential. Here are some skills that are highly valuable in Azure DevOps:

1. **Azure Services:** Gain proficiency in Azure services, as they form the backbone of many Azure DevOps solutions. Understanding services like Azure App Service, Azure Functions, and Azure Kubernetes Service (AKS) can be beneficial.
2. **Infrastructure as Code (IaC):** Learn IaC concepts and tools such as Azure Resource Manager (ARM) templates and Terraform to manage infrastructure programmatically.
3. **Scripting and Automation:** Proficiency in scripting languages like PowerShell, Bash, or Python is crucial for automating tasks and processes.
4. **Containerization:** Understand container technologies like Docker and Kubernetes, which are widely used for deploying and managing applications in Azure.
5. **CI/CD Pipelines:** Master CI/CD tools like Azure DevOps Pipelines or Jenkins to automate software delivery pipelines.
6. **Security:** Stay updated on security best practices and tools for securing Azure deployments. Knowledge of Azure Security Center and Azure Key Vault is valuable.
7. **Monitoring and Analytics:** Learn how to use monitoring and analytics tools like Azure Monitor and Application Insights to gain insights into application performance.

Networking and Community Engagement

Networking plays a significant role in career growth. Engage with the Azure DevOps community through various channels:

1. **Online Communities:** Join forums, discussion boards, and social media groups dedicated to Azure DevOps. Participate in discussions, ask questions, and share your knowledge.
2. **Conferences and Meetups:** Attend industry conferences, webinars, and local meetups to connect with peers, experts, and potential employers.
3. **Contributions:** Consider contributing to open-source projects related to Azure DevOps. Your contributions can showcase your skills and expertise.
4. **Mentorship:** Seek mentors and advisors who can provide guidance and career advice. Mentoring relationships can be invaluable for career growth.

Continuous Learning

Azure DevOps is a rapidly evolving field. To stay ahead, commit to continuous learning:

1. **Certifications:** Pursue relevant Azure and DevOps certifications to validate your skills. Microsoft offers various certifications for Azure professionals.
2. **Online Courses:** Enroll in online courses and tutorials from platforms like Microsoft Learn, Pluralsight, and edX to acquire new skills and knowledge.
3. **Books and Documentation:** Keep up with the latest books and official documentation to deepen your understanding of Azure DevOps.
4. **Experimentation:** Set up personal projects or labs to

experiment with new technologies and practices. Hands-on experience is a powerful learning tool.

5. **Stay Informed:** Follow blogs, podcasts, and news sources related to Azure and DevOps to stay informed about industry trends and updates.

Career Advancement

As you gain experience and expertise, you can explore opportunities for career advancement in Azure DevOps. Consider the following strategies:

1. **Leadership Roles:** As you become more seasoned, you may aspire to leadership positions such as DevOps Manager or Director of DevOps.
2. **Specialization:** Focus on a specific area of Azure DevOps, such as security, automation, or container orchestration, and become a subject matter expert.
3. **Consulting and Training:** Share your knowledge by offering consulting services or training sessions to organizations looking to adopt Azure DevOps practices.
4. **Entrepreneurship:** Consider starting your own consultancy or DevOps-related business if you have a unique offering or solution.
5. **Mentoring:** Give back to the community by mentoring newcomers to Azure DevOps and helping them navigate their careers.

Conclusion

A career in Azure DevOps can be both rewarding and fulfilling, provided you stay committed to learning, skill development, and community engagement. By choosing the right career path, continuously improving your skills, networking with peers, and embracing a growth mindset, you can build a successful and meaningful career in this dynamic field. Remember that Azure DevOps is not just a job; it's a journey of continuous improvement and innovation. Enjoy the ride!

Section 20.5: Final Thoughts and Encouragement for DevOps Practitioners

As we conclude this comprehensive guide to Azure DevOps, it's essential to reflect on the journey you've undertaken and provide some final thoughts and encouragement for all DevOps practitioners, whether you're just starting or have years of experience.

Celebrating Achievements

First and foremost, take a moment to celebrate your achievements. Whether you've successfully implemented CI/CD pipelines, learned new automation techniques, or improved collaboration within your team, every milestone matters. DevOps is about continuous improvement, and each step forward brings you closer to your goals.

Embracing a Growth Mindset

In the world of DevOps, change is constant. New tools, technologies, and best practices emerge regularly. Embrace a growth mindset that encourages learning and adaptation. Don't be afraid to explore unfamiliar territories and experiment with new approaches. Your ability to adapt to change will be a valuable asset throughout your career.

Learning from Failures

Failure is a natural part of the DevOps journey. Projects may encounter setbacks, deployments might fail, and issues may arise unexpectedly. However, these failures provide valuable learning experiences. Instead of dwelling on mistakes, focus on identifying root causes, implementing improvements, and preventing similar issues in the future. Failures are opportunities for growth.

Collaboration and Communication

Effective collaboration and communication are at the heart of DevOps. Continue to foster a culture of openness, transparency, and teamwork within your organization. Encourage cross-functional collaboration between development, operations, security, and other teams. Remember that DevOps is not just about tools; it's about people and processes.

Continuous Improvement

DevOps is all about continuous improvement. Regularly review and refine your processes, automation, and workflows. Seek feedback from your team and stakeholders to identify areas for enhancement. The pursuit of excellence is an ongoing journey, and there is always room for improvement.

Giving Back to the Community

Consider giving back to the DevOps community that has provided you with knowledge and support. Share your experiences, insights, and expertise with others. Contribute to open-source projects, write blog posts, or speak at conferences and meetups. By sharing your knowledge, you can help others on their DevOps journeys.

Balancing Automation and Human Touch

While automation is a fundamental aspect of DevOps, it's essential to strike a balance between automation and the human touch. Automation enhances efficiency and reduces errors, but it's people who design, implement, and maintain automation. Don't forget the importance of human creativity, problem-solving, and empathy in the DevOps equation.

Staying Informed

Stay informed about industry trends, emerging technologies, and best practices in DevOps. Subscribe to newsletters, follow industry blogs, and participate in webinars and conferences. A well-informed DevOps practitioner is better equipped to adapt to change and drive innovation.

Maintaining Work-Life Balance

Lastly, remember that a successful DevOps career should be balanced with a healthy personal life. Burnout can be a real challenge in the fast-paced world of DevOps, so prioritize self-care, downtime, and spending time with loved ones. A well-rested and rejuvenated individual is more effective in their professional endeavors.

In closing, your journey in Azure DevOps is a testament to your dedication and passion for the field. Whether you're an aspiring DevOps engineer or a seasoned professional, your contributions to the world of DevOps are invaluable. Keep learning, growing, and pushing the boundaries of what's possible. With your continued efforts, the future of DevOps looks bright, and you have the opportunity to shape it. Best of luck on your DevOps adventure!

www.ingramcontent.com/pod-product-compliance
Lightning Source LLC
LaVergne TN
LVHW090303210926
848480LV00001B/110
* 9 7 9 8 2 2 4 5 6 0 4 9 3 *